Scotland's leading educational publishers

#1 FOR REVISION

CfE Higher
PHYSICAL EDUCATION
SUCCESS GUIDE

CfE Higher PHYSICAL EDUCATION SUCCESS GUIDE

Caroline Duncan • Linda McLean

Contents

Preparing for Higher Physical Education

Section 1: Performance unit

Section 2: Factors impacting performance

Contents

Introduction

Overview of the course

Higher Physical Education is a performance development driven course that has been designed to explore the impact that the four factors – **Mental**, **Emotional**, **Social** and **Physical** – have on performance across different activities.

The units

The course consists of two units: **Performance skills** and **Factors impacting on performance**.

Throughout the Higher course you will work on developing your understanding of both the Performance skills unit and the Factors impacting on performance unit. Your prior learning during the National 5 course will aid your understanding of the factors that are developed throughout these two units.

Within these units you will develop an in-depth understanding of the key assessment standards, which at Higher level are as follows:

Performance skills		Factors impacting performance	
1	Demonstrate a broad and comprehensive range of complex movement and performance skills in physical activities:	1	Analyse and evaluate factors that impact on performance in physical activities by:
1.1	Selecting and applying a broad and comprehensive range of complex movement and performance skills, displaying a high level of control and fluency;	1.1	Analysing methods used to identify factors impacting on a performance;
		1.2	Evaluating the impact of positive and negative factors on a performance;
1.2	Demonstrating precise body and spatial awareness with distinct patterns and/or rhythms;	1.3	Explaining approaches to performance development based on these evaluations.
1.3	Working co-operatively with others;	2	Evaluate the process of personal performance development by:
1.4	Using well-established techniques, composition or tactics;	2.1	Producing a personal development plan that sets appropriate development targets;
1.5	Making appropriate decisions in challenging contexts;	2.2	Selecting methods to record and monitor development;
1.6	Reacting appropriately and making effective, safe adaptations in response to a wide range of challenging variables.	2.3	Implementing the development plan;
		2.4	Evaluating the effectiveness of the development plan and the methods used to monitor development;
		2.5	Identifying and justifying decisions relating to future personal development needs.

You will complete tasks within the units both independently and in groups. This may require you to research facts, develop your own personalised programme or make a presentation to the rest of your class.

You must pass all unit assessments in order to be presented for the full course assessment.

Overview of the course assessments

Single performance

The single performance is worth **60%** of your overall mark. The marks are distributed as follows:

Planning	8 marks
Performance	40 marks
Evaluation	12 marks
	Total 60 marks

The single performance task can be completed through an activity you are developing in school, or, if your teacher can manage the assessments appropriately, it can be completed for a personal activity you perform outwith school.

Your teacher will assess the single performance using specific assessment criteria – these are detailed on pages 10–17.

The exam

The exam is worth **40%** of your overall mark. This means 40 marks are available. The exam lasts one and a half hours.

It is split into two sections and will examine your ability to integrate and apply knowledge and understanding from across the two units which make up the course. Section one is worth 24 marks and consists of two questions on three of the factor areas.

Section two of the exam will be a 'scenario'. There are 16 marks available for this section. This will be a performance problem and may take the form of:

- graphs;
- tables;
- charts;
- a variety of other texts.

In the exam you will need to show that you can:

- analyse and explain the factors which impact on performance;
- analyse the recording, monitoring and evaluation of the process of performance development.

How to use this Success Guide

This book is intended to help you achieve the best grade possible for your Higher Physical Education course. The book is split into two main sections:

- Performance;
- Factors impacting performance.

The Performance section makes clear the criteria you must demonstrate while participating in your single performance event. This gives guidance about how skills should be applied during the performance, how control and fluency must be applied consistently and the importance of making and carrying through appropriate decisions while participating. Advice about the need for good etiquette and adherence to rules as well as controlling emotions is also given.

In the Factors impacting performance section all of the areas of mandatory content that are examinable in the final exam are covered for each of the four factors.

Exam-style questions are included throughout to test your knowledge and understanding. Detailed answer frameworks are included at the back of the book. You can use these templates to construct your answers, making them personal to you and the activities you have studied. The missing sections, indicted by '...', are where you should add information related to your own experiences in order to gain the full range of marks available.

Section 1
Performance Unit

This chapter is intended to help you prepare for the Performance unit assessment and the single performance event for the course assessment. This will involve learning and developing a range of movement and performance skills and being able to apply them to activities effectively.

During the Higher course you may have the opportunity to try out a range of physical activities, however, you must provide evidence of assessment in two physical activities.

You will be assessed during a practical performance and will have to demonstrate a broad and comprehensive range of complex performance skills in both of your selected physical activities. You can be assessed within any realistic experience, situation or conditioned activity. This evidence may be collected over a period of time, which will allow you to work on the consistency, fluency and effectiveness of your performance.

You may decide to use one of these activities for the course assessment in performance – the single performance.

Performance skills

In order to successfully complete the Performance skills unit you will have to achieve all of the assessment standards.

The diagrams on the following pages give more detail on each assessment standard. They are followed by examples from a range of activities.

1.1 Selecting and applying a broad and comprehensive range of complex movement and performance skills, displaying a high level of control and fluency

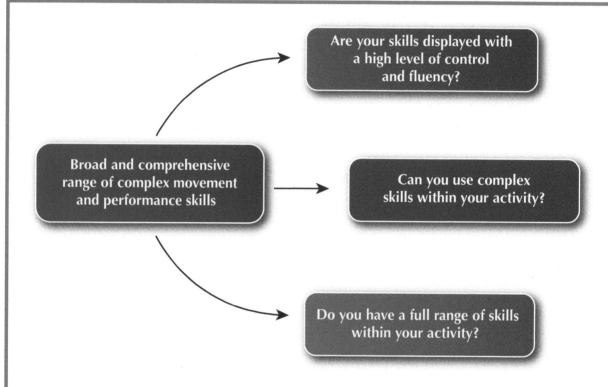

Broad and comprehensive range of complex movement and performance skills

Are your skills displayed with a high level of control and fluency?

Can you use complex skills within your activity?

Do you have a full range of skills within your activity?

Examples
Football

The performer should have a full range of different skills, both simple and complex. For example, in football the performer should be able to show complex skills such as a volley, as well as fluently demonstrate more simple skills, such as an inside pass along the ground. They should be able to link and combine skills together smoothly, showing that they are in control. They should be able to move fluently with or without the ball, changing pace and direction, and be able to pass effectively on the move and take scoring opportunities.

Gymnastics

The performer will have a full range of gymnastic skills, including rotation, flight, inversion and balance. They are able to perform more complex skills such as a handstand into forward roll, which is completed with smooth, fluent links. The range of skills can be applied to perform different sequences or on apparatus.

Tennis

The performer will have a full and wide selection of shots they are able to play, both complex and simple. Effective use of both backhand and forehand shots will be evident, as well as effective serve and volley. Shots will be played effortlessly and be smooth flowing.

1.2 Demonstrating precise body and spatial awareness with distinct patterns and/or rhythms

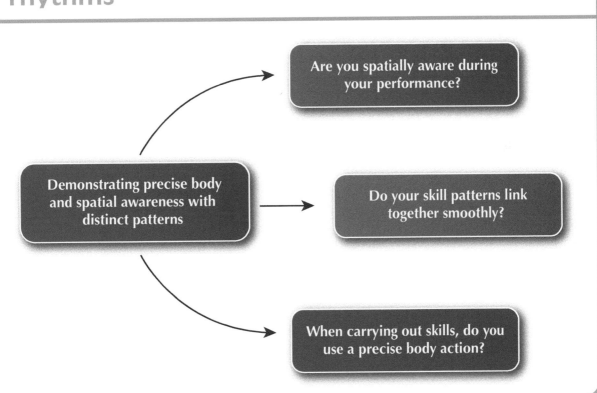

Demonstrating precise body and spatial awareness with distinct patterns

Are you spatially aware during your performance?

Do your skill patterns link together smoothly?

When carrying out skills, do you use a precise body action?

Examples
Football

The performer should be able to co-ordinate their body actions when carrying out skills, so that they achieve accuracy and success. When passing the ball the muscles and joints in the leg must be used effectively for success. The performer should always be aware of other players around them and where to position themselves for successful outcomes both in attack and defence. Linking skilled patterns, such as running with the ball to passing out wide, should be smooth.

Gymnastics

The performer must be able to co-ordinate their body actions, so that they can use the joints and muscles effectively to achieve a particular skill. When performing a handstand they must transfer their weight forward and downward in one movement in order to successfully hold it. During a sequence performance they should use all of the space, showing different directions and levels. During a floor routine, they must show smooth linking patterns between movements to achieve a good performance.

Tennis

The performer must co-ordinate their body actions to generate power and accuracy and place shots at different parts of the court. This will require accurate timing of leg and arm actions. The performer must be aware of space so that they can attack open spaces in the court.

1.3 Working co-operatively with others

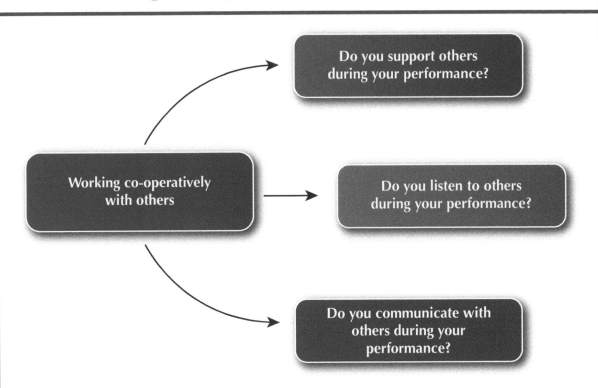

Working co-operatively with others

Do you support others during your performance?

Do you listen to others during your performance?

Do you communicate with others during your performance?

Examples

Football

The performer must be able to speak to fellow teammates and work effectively as a unit. The performer needs to listen to teammates, especially when supporting in defence or attack. For example, in a counter-attack, midfield players need to move forward in support of the attackers.

Gymnastics

The performer must be able to communicate with other gymnasts and coaches, especially during more challenging routines or when working on apparatus. Being able to share ideas about routines and application of skills is essential when designing a performance. For example, the performer and their coach may discuss the best possible techniques in order to gain the most marks.

Tennis

During a doubles match the performer must constantly listen to and share tactics with their partner. It is crucial they work together when deciding on an opening tactic. Support must be shown to a partner, especially when motivation is required.

1.4 Using well-established techniques, composition or tactics

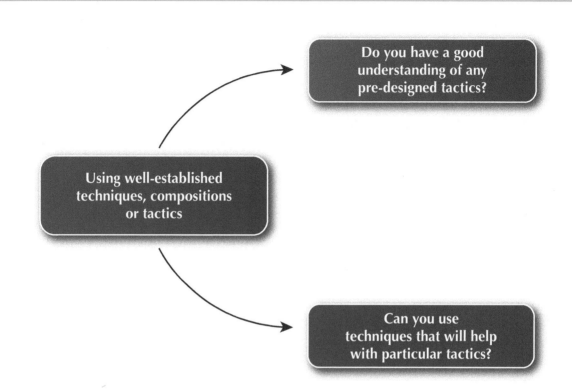

Examples
Football

The performer must be able to successfully use techniques which aid in the completion of specific tactics. In a set piece, the performer will know the techniques they have to apply for their particular role. During a corner, the performer must be able to cross the ball into the desired area for the tactic to be successful. They must be fully aware of any offensive or defensive tactic and what their role and responsibility is within that tactic.

Gymnastics

When designing routines, the performer must be able to use specific techniques, which allow the space or the apparatus to be used effectively. For example, during a vault the performer should use challenging techniques, such as a handspring vault, to try to achieve the best possible marks. The performer should be prepared in advance.

Tennis

The performer must be able to serve a variety of shots at his opponent, for example, a slice serve to take the player wide out of court or a serve into the body to 'tuck him up' and restrict freedom of movement in his return. The performer should go into the performance with pre-thought-out tactics, which he can effectively use against a specific opponent.

1.5 Making appropriate decisions in challenging contexts

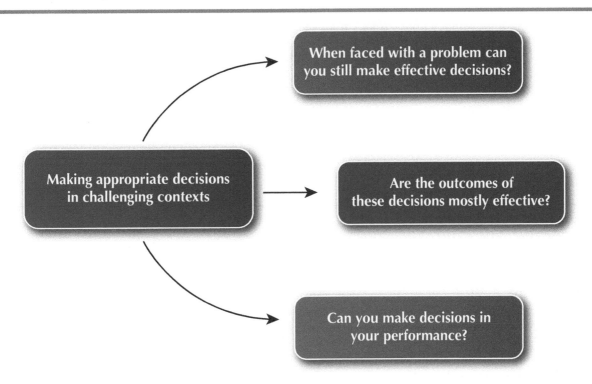

Examples
Football

The performer must be able to make a variety of decisions during a performance, for example, deciding when to pass to a teammate or when to make a challenge on the ball. The performer should also be able to make challenging decisions during specific attacking and defensive situations, e.g. making a through pass in a counter-attack or making the decision to sit back in defence.

Gymnastics

The performer must be able to decide on the correct types of skill to use during their floor routine or apparatus work. They must also decide what complexity of skill is required to achieve appropriate marks. This may involve the performer adding a more complex skill, such as a handstand forward roll, to gain more marks. They must also decide on the correct floor patterns to use during their floor routine to ensure their performance is effective.

Tennis

The performer must be able to make quick decisions regarding the type and placement of the next shot. Decisions will also be made about the type of tactic the performer may want to use against an opponent. These decisions must be made in challenging contexts, such as deciding where is best to place a ball in the court to win a point. For example, being caught tight to the net and playing a deep lob into the back of the court.

1.6 Reacting appropriately and making effective, safe adaptations in response to a wide range of challenging variables

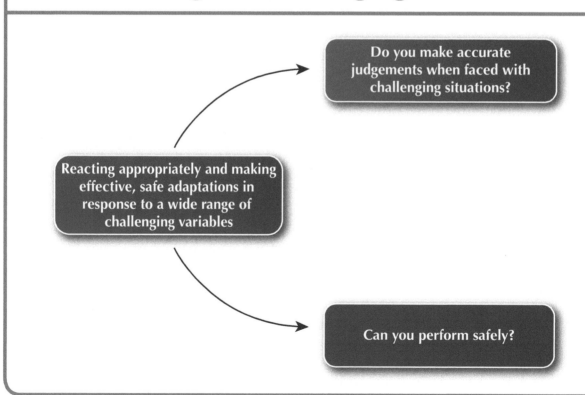

Do you make accurate judgements when faced with challenging situations?

Reacting appropriately and making effective, safe adaptations in response to a wide range of challenging variables

Can you perform safely?

Examples
Football

The performer must be able to perform safely within the environment of the game. They must be aware of potentially challenging situations, such as late tackles, which may result in injury to themselves or others. When a challenge is made on the ball they must be able to complete this safely and within the rules and sportsmanship of the game.

Gymnastics

The performer must be aware of any safety challenges in relation to the apparatus or other performers when performing in group situations. They must be aware that particular skills have safety risks and therefore be confident that they can perform these skills effectively or look for support. For example, during a vault, the performer must be confident that they can complete a handspring with or without support.

Tennis

The performer must be aware of the different conditions that they may have to play in. Consideration must be given to the playing surface and how this may impact their performance, so that injury can be avoided. For example, wet grass may lead to a potential slip hazard, therefore the performer should be aware of this and adapt their play accordingly.

Performance course assessment

The Performance aspect of your course assessment is worth **60%** of your final grade. 8 marks are allocated for how you plan for your single performance, 40 marks for the actual performance and 12 marks for the evaluation of your performance. During this performance you will be given the opportunity to demonstrate the skills, knowledge and understanding detailed in the following pages.

Planning stage

TOP TIPS

Criteria for successful single performance	
Explain the relevance of two challenges you will face in this single performance	• Make sure you have plenty of time to prepare for your single performance, so that you can create a plan for the specific challenges you will encounter. • Think about setting yourself short- and long-term goals. • Your goals need to be realistic and co-ordinated so that you can achieve your best.
Explain how you will prepare to meet these challenges	• You need to make sure that the approaches and training programme you design have been clearly thought out. • Make sure you give yourself enough time to meet the challenges you have set yourself. • Approach your challenges with clear aims. • The approaches you use must be appropriate to the activity. • You may have to change or adapt your approaches, depending on the situations.

Examples

Dance

During my routine/motif, I feel I have not used a variety of different travel floor paths. I used a lot of straight pathways, which do not effectively use the space available. Therefore one of my challenges will be to add a combination of curved and straight lines, so that my performance looks more effective to the audience, and because these floor patterns will allow me to use different motifs, which will add to the presentation of my performance.

Using a variety of floor patterns, such as diagonal lines, circle formations and spirals, will help me to communicate the message of my composition.

My second challenge will be to look at different levels in my composition, as currently my performance is very much on one level. Exploring different levels will show a wider range of creativity in my movement and motif patterns. I can explore using high, medium and low levels through kneeling, standing, jumping or lying down.

Netball

As a goal attack, I am sometimes unable to get free to receive a pass which allows me to shoot or pass when attacking. My first challenge is to make myself more available to receive a pass, by deceiving my marker and getting into a free space. My second challenge is to work on my timing on getting free to receive the pass, so that I don't leave it too late, resulting in a mis-pass.

Badminton

During my performance, I am very aware that when forced onto my backhand, I am unable to play an efficient shot to either capitalise on my opponent's mistake or play a defensive shot to the back court. My two main challenges are my inability to move my feet quickly enough to get into position and also the timing and direction of my shot. This results in me either mis-hitting the shuttle or not generating enough power to put my opponent under pressure.

Implementing stage

You must be assessed in a challenging, competitive and/or demanding situation. For example, a final dance performance or a football tournament.

You will need to show skills, knowledge and understanding that will show you:

- selecting, demonstrating and safely applying a broad and comprehensive range of complex movement and performance skills in challenging contexts;
- making decisions and solving problems in challenging contexts.

Marks will be allocated in the following areas of your performance:

TOP TIP

- Make sure you have given yourself enough time to plan for your single performance.
- Whether you intend to train using different approaches or you intend to change or adapt within your performance, make sure you have clearly highlighted how you hope to overcome your challenges.
- Have a clear and appropriate timescale for your performance – discuss this with your teacher.

Assessment item	0 marks	1–2 mark range	3–4 mark range	5–6 mark range	7–8 mark range
2 (a) Performance repertoire	Shows no evidence of a basic performance repertoire.	Applies a basic performance repertoire consistently.	Applies a **broad** performance repertoire, selecting and combining some complex skills appropriately to meet the demands of the performance context.	Applies a broad and **well-established** performance repertoire, selecting and combining some complex skills **effectively** to meet the demands of the performance context.	Applies a broad and well-established performance repertoire **consistently**, selecting and combining complex skills effectively to meet the demands of the performance context.
2 (b) Control and fluency	Shows no evidence of control and fluency during the performance.	Control and fluency usually demonstrated during the performance, while unchallenged.	Control and fluency usually demonstrated during the performance while responding with **variable effectiveness** to challenges.	Control and fluency usually demonstrated during the performance while responding **effectively** to challenges.	Control and fluency **consistently** demonstrated during the performance while responding effectively to challenges.

Assessment item	0 marks	1–2 mark range	3–4 mark range	5–6 mark range	7–8 mark range
2 (c) *Decision-making and problem-solving throughout the performance*	Shows no evidence of appropriate decision-making skills.	Demonstrates appropriate decision-making skills in response to a range of straightforward performance demands throughout the performance.	Demonstrates **appropriate decision-making** skills in response to a range of challenging performance demands throughout the performance.	Demonstrates ability to make appropriate decisions **quickly** in response to a range of challenging performance demands throughout the performance.	Demonstrates ability to **anticipate** and make appropriate decisions quickly in response to a range of challenging performance demands throughout the performance.
2 (d) *The effectiveness of following through on the decision-making*	Shows no evidence of effectiveness in following through on decision-making during the performance.	Following through on decision-making results in limited effectiveness **occasionally** during the performance.	Following through on decision-making results in limited effectiveness **throughout** the performance.	Following through on decision-making results in **effectiveness throughout** the performance.	Following through on decision-making results in effectiveness throughout the performance, especially in response to **challenging demands**.
2 (e) *Following rules and regulations and displaying etiquette during the performance*	Shows no evidence of following rules and regulations or displaying appropriate etiquette.	Follows rules and regulations and displays appropriate etiquette occasionally during the performance.	Follows rules and regulations and displays appropriate etiquette at the start of, during, and at the end of the performance.		
2 (f) *Control of emotions during the performance*	Shows no evidence of controlling emotions during the performance.	Demonstrates control of emotions occasionally during the performance.	Demonstrates control of emotions throughout the performance.		

Here are some examples of how the above assessment criteria could be applied to activities:

	Dance	Netball	Badminton
Demonstrating a broad and comprehensive performance repertoire (including movement and performance skills during the performance)	• Are you able to use a variety of travelling movements, such as running jumping, skipping, leaping? • Can you use different styles of dynamic movement pattern?	• Do you have a full range of skills, such as passing and receiving, movement off the ball, tracking, pivoting?	• Do you have a full skills repertoire, such as overhead clears, smash, drive, drop shot, variety of serves?
Demonstrate control and fluency of complex movement and performance skills during the performance	• Are you able to link different motifs fluently and seamlessly? • Do you use complex movement skills, such as stag leaps?	• Are your actions fluent? • Can you receive and pass successfully in one fluent movement? • Are you able to fluently lose your marker to receive a pass, with the correct timing?	• Do you show smooth movement patterns around the court? • Are you able to fluently link actions together to produce an effective shot? • Within your skill repertoire, are you able to use some complex skills, such as clearing from the back court?
Demonstrate decision-making and problem-solving throughout the performance	• Have you been able to use the available floor space effectively? For example, do you use different levels or directions of pathways? • Have you been able to solve problems within the performance, such as repeating movements too often?	• What types of decisions do you make during your performance? • Do you make good decisions when passing the ball to your teammates, for example, passing early, when teammate is unmarked? • Do you make good decisions when deciding to play a particular centre pass strategy? This may require passing to the wing defence, when the wing attack is double marked.	• Are you able to make the correct shot decisions when trying to out-manoeuvre your opponent? • Are you aware of the decisions you make to exploit your opponent's weaknesses? • Are you able to make decisions when deciding to attack or play a defensive shot, such as clearing the shuttle to the back court?

	Dance	Netball	Badminton
Demonstrate the effectiveness of following through on the decision-making process during the performance	• Have you been successful in the decisions you have made? • Have they successfully added to the performance?	• Do your decisions lead to a positive outcome in your performance? • Do they lead to a goal being scored? • Do they lead to space being opened out in the centre third?	• Do your decisions lead to positive outcomes in your performance? • Do they lead to a point being scored or to playing an effective defensive shot? • Do they lead to space being exploited that you can capitalise on?
Demonstrate the following rules and regulations and display etiquette during the performance	• Have you been able to perform within the set time and work with others, whether a teacher or classmate? • Have you been able to work out different motifs through discussing and compromising with your dance partner?	• Are you able to play within the rules and regulations of the game, making sure you understand the court positioning and the foot fault rules? • Do you show support to your teammates? • Do you consider fair play during your performance?	• Are you able to play within the rules and regulations of the game, making sure you understand the court lines, the service box, the scoring rules for Singles or Doubles? • Do you understand net faults? • Do you show support to your Doubles partner? • Do you clearly discuss the tactics you might use? • Are you considerate to your opponent, e.g. handing back the shuttlecock?
Demonstrate control of emotions during the performance	• Have you been able to keep control of any anxiety or nervousness during your performance? • Are these emotions hidden during your performance?	• Are you able to control your emotions during a situation when the umpire may call against you? • Are you able to control your frustration when your teammates let you down?	• Are you able to control your emotions after playing an unsuccessful shot? • Does your head go down after playing poorly? • Do you lose control of your racket or start to kick the shuttle?

Evaluating stage

TOP TIPS

Analyse the effectiveness of your preparation for the two challenges explained in the planning stage	• What information do you have that proves whether the challenges have been met or not? • Is this based on objective (quantitative) or subjective (qualitative) information? • Can you back up your response with data from comparisons? • Think about using before and after performances.
Evaluate at least one strength and at least one area for development from your performance	• Look back at your performance and identify what worked and what did not. • Make sure you have identified one strength and one area for future development. • Make sure you relate this to how they will impact performance. • You must present an overall judgment of what your performance now looks like, using the data you have collected.

Examples

Dance

After addressing my challenges, my one-off performance in Dance was an effective composition. Before addressing my challenges, I found that I used too many straight patterns in my performance, which were completed very much at the same floor level. This can be seen from the subjective profile that my dance teacher gave back to me. I have developed my performance through adding a combination of floor patterns, such as curved patterns which lead into straight formations. This gives the audience a more effective visual performance. By adding different floor levels, through kneeling, standing, jumping or lying down, my performance has a new dynamic, which allows me to use choreographic devices more effectively.

Netball

After addressing my challenges, my one-off performance in Netball is more effective. During my performance I can apply a variety of different methods to lose my marker and make myself available for a pass. From watching my performance in the first quarter, we successfully made 15 out of 20 received passes without my marker being able to intercept, allowing me to effectively pass and move during our attacking strategy. I found that my 2 v1 and 3 v2 practices made me really think about the movement patterns I had to use to make myself available for a pass. During these practices I also took into account the timing of my movement and how I used different speeds to lose my markers. This allowed me to use the correct time to pass and move.

Badminton

After addressing my challenges, my one-off performance in Badminton has shown some effectiveness. Before addressing my challenges I found that I rarely moved into position before playing any backhand shots. During my one-off performance, I was able to move from my ready position into my preparation position in 14 out of my 20 backhand clears. This allowed me to carry out the shot far more effectively, as I was able to contact the shuttle at its top point, allowing the racket to speed through the shuttle to generate more power. This allowed me to clear the shuttle high over my opponent towards the backcourt and therefore defend on my backhand (so not setting up an attacking shot for my opponent to capitalise on). This movement now allows me to correctly time my shot, which again will generate more power and allow me to force my opponent to the backcourt. This helps me get into a more attacking position.

Section 2
Factors impacting performance

This section is intended to help you prepare for the final exam. This will involve learning and developing knowledge, understanding and skills.

In the exam, you will have to demonstrate application of the mandatory skills, knowledge and understanding.

They can be broken down into three separate parts:

Part 1 – Methods of collecting information to analyse factors impacting on performance

Part 2 – Approaches to performance development

Part 3 – Recording, monitoring and evaluating performance development

For all of these areas you may be asked:
To describe, to explain, to analyse or to evaluate the knowledge or skills you have developed throughout your course. These are **competencies** you will develop across all Higher courses.

This will allow you to apply these skills and knowledge to help you solve different performance problems.

We will work through each area for the different factors and for all four **competencies**.

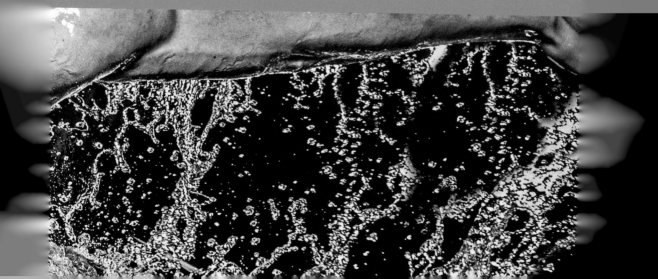

Command words in Physical Education

Thinking skills in PE

All parts of your course are designed to encourage you to become:

1. Successful learners
2. Effective contributors
3. Responsible citizens
4. Confident individuals

In PE your experiences taking part in activities which form part of your course and in activities you do after or outside school will help you develop physical, emotional, mental and social skills. The processes you go through and the knowledge you gain will help you complete all parts of the internal unit assessments and the course assessments.

The range of thinking skills you will develop will be common to many of your Higher courses. This will help you to make connections between different subjects and to use skills in both familiar and unfamiliar situations. By doing this you can begin to understand different concepts and move towards being successful in all aspects of your learning.

It is important to understand that the thinking skills you will develop while studying this course will indeed challenge you to THINK. Sometimes you might only need to *describe* – give details about what something looks like. At other times you will need to *explain* – give reasons why something is the way it is. Analysing at Higher is another skill you will develop. This will require you to break down methods of collecting information, information you gather, approaches you use to develop performance and the tools you use to monitor and evaluate the personal development plan. When asked to *evaluate* you are being asked to look at the advantages and disadvantages and to assess or measure the progress you made towards developing your performance. Judgements need to be made about how useful the process you carried out actually was.

These are *command words*. They tell you what *type of thinking* you need to do to show your understanding of the performance development process.

Throughout your unit assessment and course assessment (exam) you will come across these command words telling you to do something with the knowledge you have. When you understand what these words mean you will be able to answer the questions well and achieve high marks.

Describing

This skill asks you to tell the reader:

- what a performance looks like;
- what strengths are demonstrated in the performance;
- what the development needs are.

The description should include details, more than just a statement. Consideration could be given to including details as follows:

Physical factor — fitness	Improved by adding
I was slow to the ball. 	I was slow to the ball, arriving after my opponent, who got there 9 times out of 10 before me.

Physical factor — skill	
My arm was bent. 	My arm was bent as I struck the shuttle above and in front of my head.

Physical factor — tactics/composition	
The outlet pass was made. 	The outlet pass was made quickly and powerfully right out to the far side of the court away from the opposition.

Mental factor

I made bad decisions.	I made three bad decisions in the first four minutes of play, putting the ball out of play twice, and giving possession to the opposition as I tried to dribble when I should have passed

Emotional factor

I panicked when I landed badly	I panicked when I landed badly from my front somersault, ending up facing a quarter turn around from where I needed to be to begin my run up for my handspring.

Social factor

The crowd intimidated me.	The crowd intimidated me and made me hesitate as I moved forward to begin serving to win the match.

Summary – include as much detail as possible about what it is you are describing. Try to keep in mind that you are trying to paint a picture or provide a commentary for someone who has not seen the performance, method of data collection, approach you used or monitoring/evaluating tool.

Explaining

This skill asks you to tell the reader:

- why you did what you did;
- the relationship between decisions you took and the difference this made.

Explaining means using linking words such as, 'I did this …

- because …
- so that …
- in order to allow me to …
- to make sure that …
- to provide me with the opportunity to …
- when I needed to …'

By adding these details to an explanation the reader can see what was done and why it was done. This is called cause and effect. An easy way to remember to link cause and effect is:

Cause	Effect
I lost my watch	I was late for school
I didn't study for my exam	I failed the exam
I let my opponent get away from me	She scored a goal
I was too slow with my run-up	I took off from the wrong place

Analysing

This skill asks you to tell the reader:

- what parts are important in a method, information or an approach;
- if there are connections between methods, information or approaches.

Analysing means using phrases like:

- This shows me that …
- This allowed for …
- As a result …
- This resulted in …
- The result of this course of action was …
- This meant that …

Analysing means you have to deconstruct, take apart and make clear the different parts of the methods of data collection, the approaches used, the strengths and weaknesses within your performance and the methods you used to monitor and evaluate the progress you made.

You should be able to analyse areas from all three sections of the mandatory content:

1. Methods of data collection – allows accurate collection of information, which results in easily interpreted data … This shows strengths and weaknesses clearly … as a result you were able to start planning based on …

2. Approaches – the approach used resulted in improved back stroke in the preparation and action stages … this meant I had a longer, deeper pull … giving more propulsion …

3. Methods to monitor and evaluate – these show me that the weakness has reduced from 18/30 failed attempts to 6/30. This indicates that my methods gave me data …

Evaluating

This skill asks you to tell the reader:

*   **how** successful or otherwise was the method or approach you used.

Evaluating means using phrases like:

*   demonstrating a significant improvement …
*   clearly, results show …
*   overall the preferred method would be … because …
*   the approach most useful was … because …

A value or judgement has to be made when evaluating something. You need to determine how useful, appropriate or effective your methods or approaches were. Also, if you were asked to evaluate your performance it might be a good idea to try and include some evidence to back up your judgements about what was:

*   best – proved by the percentage increase in your number of successful serves;
*   worst – highlighted by the lack of motivation you felt while carrying out your training;
*   more useful – than another method based on the ease of using the method to gather information;
*   less productive – based on the scores of your last match where you lost.

You might want to use the following value words:

*   Outstanding
*   Excellent
*   Very good
*   Average
*   Below average

These words give you the opportunity to back up the judgement you make.

Analysing information collection methods

The key issues in this topic are:

- **P**racticability – about carrying out a process which is feasible, possible to organise or put into practice.
- **A**ppropriateness – about the suitability of the method. That is, is the test 'fit for purpose'?
- **R**eliability – about gathering information which can be trusted.
- **V**alidity – about gathering information which can be defended, and is credible and sound.

When we set out to analyse the impact factors can have on performance we must keep these issues in mind. By doing this we can be sure that what we intend to measure is actually measured.

Practicability and organisational issues

If the method requires specialist equipment or is practically complicated to set out then it is possible that mistakes could be made. This could mean that the information collected might not be accurate, reliable or valid. For example, if a tape measure was not used to set out the Leger Test, then it is possible that results for those using a longer or shorter running area could not be used for comparison purposes. For example, if your score of 67 when running the 20m Leger Test were to be compared with that of someone who had run the test over only 18m and achieved 68, then the comparisons would not be fair.

Appropriateness of data collection methods

You must make sure the test chosen for performance analysis suits the activity and the factor you are investigating. For example, an Illinois Agility Test would not give useful information about the number of successful passes a hockey player made on the move with the ball. The Hoff Test for stamina in footballers is a very specific test for players who have a good skill level and can complete the variety of 'stations' to a high degree. It would not be appropriate to use this test with players who could not dribble or pass the ball.

Therefore, you must be clear about the area of your performance you wish to collect information on, as only then can an appropriate method be identified and put into use. The methods should be practicable – easy to carry out; appropriate – match the need of the feature being measured; reliable – not open to errors; and produce valid results which tell us about 'how weak our weakness is'.

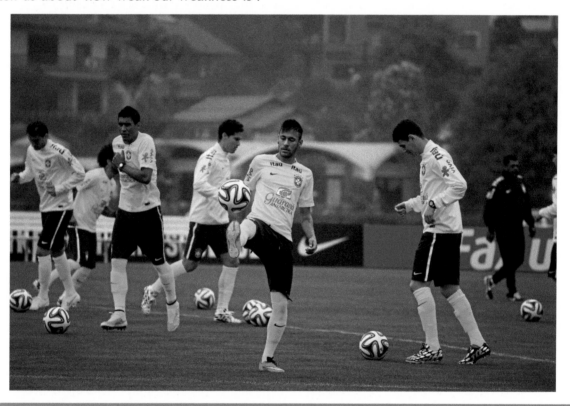

Reliability and validity

If the method can be carried out the same way time after time then it is likely that the results collected can be trusted. This means the person who carries out the observation schedule and the conditions under which the observations are gathered must remain as 'constant' as possible. By trying to set up the same conditions and people to carry out observations, then it is likely that when retesting information can be compared easily. This makes sure the results are reliable and valid and can be used to go ahead with performance development.

Summary

Remember:

P – Practical   R – Reliable

A – Appropriate   V – Valid

Mental, e.g. Bio feedback and SCAT

P – The availability and organisation of computers and scientific equipment would be a consideration for some methods used for this factor.

A – The method chosen must suit the feature and enable the performer to work in isolation if privacy is required.

R – As mental factors are affected by moods, the time of day the test is carried out must be the same for pre- and post-testing.

V – Results are valid if the performer has taken care to minimise any external influences (such as someone else being present) when tests are done.

Emotional, e.g. Disciplinary record and coach feedback

P – One practical problem is that disciplinary records are not easily accessible for performers. Coach feedback may only be given right after a performance when emotions are running high and details might not be remembered.

A – Sometimes these methods do not 'capture' the whole performance problem and so might not be appropriate, e.g. SCAT looks closely at anxiety but does not perhaps give a lot of information on lowered tolerance.

R – Care must be taken to note who is officiating and coaching. If this changes then the results might not be able to be compared easily.

V – Depending on who is giving feedback or which particular person is officiating, results might be affected by people rather than the performer.

Social, e.g. Questionnaire and self-appraisal

P – To achieve honest, accurate results, time must be set aside for methods to be carried out without being rushed.

A – Questions asked must be easily understood and the performer must feel comfortable with being honest in the self-appraisal in order that a clear starting point can be established.

R – Questions and comments recorded should allow for easy interpretation of results. This makes comparisons possible. Closed questions – those which allow yes or no answers – are good ways to get useful information.

V – Results in these two methods are not useful if the person has not answered honestly.

Physical, e.g. Standardised test and PAR sheets

P – Equipment needs to be set out perfectly, as the protocol states. Sometimes PAR is difficult to see clearly without accurate video footage.

A – The correct test must be used to measure the right area of fitness. The PAR sheet must have the skill broken down into its component parts.

R – Reliable results can be obtained if the test is set out exactly the way it states in the protocol. PAR should be used in conjunction with video to ensure analysis can be double checked.

V – Recorders are necessary and have to be clear about what their role is and what exactly they are looking for to ensure results are valid.

In the exam you might be asked to:

- **describe** how you might practically carry out a method to collect information on a factor;
- **explain** how this method was reliable and valid;
- **analyse** the practicability of the methods you used to gather data on the impact of a particular factor on performance;
- **evaluate** the reliability and appropriateness of the methods you used.

When **describing** you must give clear details about what the method was. This has to include details of its component parts, the main features of the method and the steps you went through to carry out the test.

When **explaining** how the method was reliable and valid you must give details about why the test has set rules and why it is carried out the same way each time. Also, were the results trustworthy and easy to interpret?

When **analysing** the practicability of the methods used you must give details about which parts of the test were straightforward to set up and which were not. Also how easy or difficult was it to carry out the test? Was specialised equipment required, and did this help the reliability or validity of the test?

When **evaluating** the reliability of the methods used, you need to make an overall judgement about how valuable the methods were in helping you produce information or evidence that identified areas which required attention. Overall, you must state clearly if the methods suited the factor you were examining and whether you would recommend their use to others who were investigating this factor.

Exam-style questions

1. Compare two different methods of data collection from within one factor:

   a. Describe the two methods. **(4 marks)**

   b. Explain what makes them different or more useful. **(4 marks)**

   c. Analyse why one method is better than the other. **(4 marks)**

   d. Evaluate the overall reliability of both. **(4 marks)**

TOP TIP

By being able to apply knowledge about ONE method of collecting information to make comparisons with other methods you are applying your knowledge in a different way. This shows 'deeper' learning and is a skill which will help you in the set questions and scenario parts of the exam.

Applying recognised tests or analytical tools

This assessment standard requires you to select tests or methods of analysis to gather information on performance. The recognised tests available are varied and, depending on which factor you are investigating, use different equipment or formats.

Some of the tests you might use are:

Factor	Test/method	Information collected
Physical (skill)	French low serve test	Effectiveness of low service.
Physical (fitness)	Illinois agility test	Measurement of agility.
Physical (tactics)	Match analysis sheet	Success of penalty corners.
Mental	Questionnaire	Level of arousal before, during and after a performance.
Emotional	Bio feedback	The physiological and emotional changes experienced before, during and after a performance.
Social	Environmental checklist	The availability of different training facilities within a performer's community.

For each test you would need to be sure about the rules or 'protocols' required for the setting-up and administering of each of the tests. These would ensure the results were practicable, appropriate, reliable and valid. The protocols make sure:

> Distances, times for the tests are applied.

> Equipment used is appropriate.

> Formats or formulas for calculating information are followed.

If a method is dependent on a person observing the performance, then you should make sure:

- The observer is knowledgeable about the activity in order that they have some experience to be able to complete the checklist or schedule accurately. For example, they must know if a spike is effective or not.

- That the same observer is used in any subsequent observations to make sure the observations can be compared. For example, it would be helpful to work with someone who has the same level of experience and knowledge about the activity being observed, and is able to look at your performance over a period of time.

- The observer is familiar with the method being used to collect information. This makes sure they, for example, put ticks or crosses where required and are clear about what to do as they watch the performance.

- A recording of the performance is made. This allows the observer to complete any checklists or schedules while re-watching the performance. By using the slow motion and rewind facilities, a more reliable system for collecting information can be set up. This means the information gathered is likely to provide very accurate results upon which performance development can be planned.

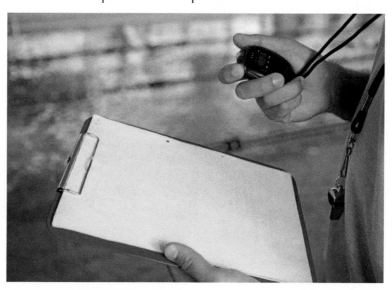

Summary

Mental	Emotional
In this factor area, questionnaires are used to assess the effects of the mental factor on performance. These questionnaires should: • measure the area they need to analyse, e.g. Profile of Mood Status (PoMS) Test; • use a medium which suits the performer, e.g. online, on paper, an interview; • use a mixture of questions to gain qualitative and quantitative information; • be short and concise.	Bio feedback, for example, is an analytical tool that uses scientific equipment and requires the performer to have a certain amount of technical knowledge, e.g. a heart-rate monitor requires the performer to know how to set it up in order to get accurate data.
Social	**Physical**
Using an environmental checklist will require features of the performer's environment to be listed and compared to similar communities, towns or cities. Comparisons are only possible if the population and social setting are within the same type of social and economic background.	Standardised tests, such as the Leger, Illinois or Cooper tests, are excellent ways to gather information on fitness, skills or the success of tactics or compositions. Protocols must be followed accurately when applying these tests or tools. This makes sure that on re-testing results can be compared and improvements in performance identified.

In the exam you might be asked to:
- **describe** the protocols for methods of information collection;
- **explain** how the protocols ensure information is valid and reliable;
- **analyse** the methods you used to gather data on the impact of a particular factor on performance;
- **evaluate** the reliability and appropriateness of the methods you used.

When **describing** you must give clear details about what the protocols were and the steps you went through to carry out the test correctly.

When **explaining** how the method was reliable and valid you must give details about why the test has set rules and why it is carried out the same way each time. Also, were the results trustworthy and easy to interpret?

When **analysing** the application of the methods used you must give details about which parts of the test were straightforward to set up and which were not. Also, how easy or difficult was it to carry out the test? Was specialised equipment required and did this help the reliability or validity of the test?

When **evaluating** the reliability of the methods used, you need to make an overall judgement about how valuable the methods were in helping you produce information or evidence that identified areas which required attention. Overall, you must state clearly if the methods suited the factor you were examining and whether you would recommend their use to others who were investigating this factor.

Exam-style questions

1. Describe the 'protocol' for a test you have used to gather information on a factor which affects your performance. **(4 marks)**

2. Explain the advantages of having an experienced observer collect information on your performance. **(4 marks)**

3. Justify the need to follow set protocols when gathering information on performance. **(4 marks)**

4. Identify two methods you have used to collect information on your performance for different factors. **(2 marks)**

5. Evaluate the benefits of both methods in enabling you to collect information that allowed you to begin planning performance development. **(6 marks)**

Model performances

Model performances help us identify what our performance **should** be like. When we watch a model performance we can generally see:

- Successful, fault-free execution of skills.
  This means there are few mistakes and each skill performance would look almost effortless. Energy used would be minimum, with maximum efficiency.

- High levels of the required aspects of fitness.
  There is nothing lacking in terms of fitness. The model performer does not display low levels of any aspect of skill or physical fitness.

- Understanding and application of correct tactical or compositional considerations.
  The model performer carries out any duties associated with his/her role confidently and successfully. She is in the right place at the right time, marking, defending, attacking and using the correct amount of lightness in a specific motif when required.

- Appropriate management of emotions.
  The model performer does not lose control of emotions, even when stressed. Top-level performers often miss this vital component of their performance and it can prove very costly at times when they really need to be focused.

- Effective decision-making, concentration, level of arousal and mental toughness.
  Mentally, an MP can make good decisions throughout her performance. This means mistakes are unlikely. She also goes into performances knowing that she will need to overcome performance problems and show great mental toughness when under pressure. This does not faze her and she seems to enjoy the challenge of the tough performance environment. Her level of arousal is always therefore under her control.

- Effective teamwork, communication, co-operation and fair play.
  Due to being totally in control of his emotions and understanding what he is required to do, he works well in groups and can communicate, co-operate and obey the rules while still giving an effective performance.

Summary

Mental	Emotional
Model performers do not always exemplify the type of mental ability we would all aspire to have. However, setting this aside, model performers demonstrate high levels of concentration, successful decision-making, problem-solving and mental toughness against which performance can be compared. Therefore the criteria they provide allow performance targets to be set.	Again, model performers are human and at times their emotions run out of control. However, the most successful model performers are those who can remain in focus when the pressure comes against them. Often when model performers' emotions are tested, they can take control. They regain calm, become less frustrated and do not panic. With this, emotions settle and optimism and creativity are encouraged.

Social	Physical
Teams or groups with high levels of self-respect and a positive team ethos make performance look effortless and easy. This leads to each person carrying out their role effectively, few disagreements and rules and codes of conduct respected and applied.	High levels of fitness, skill and understanding of role-related demands are all characteristics of a model performer. Timing is efficient and energy is not wasted. This ensures a high level of accuracy and consistency throughout a performance.

In the exam you might be asked to:

- **describe** your performance in comparison to a model performance;
- **explain** how model performances have a role to play in helping you improve your performance;
- **analyse** your own performance using criteria from a model performance;
- **evaluate** the success of the model performance.

When **describing** you must give clear details about what your performance looked like and also what the MP looked like. This should be more than a statement of 'he can do this, I can't do that …'. Details of the criteria and their effect on performance should be developed to give a picture of how the two performances differed.

When **explaining** how the MP can be used when planning and carrying out a performance development plan you must give details about the process you went though to work towards achieving the same standards as the MP.

When **analysing** the model performance and your own performance in comparison it would be useful to try to say *how much* higher their percentage success was in comparison to yours, *how much* more effective their movements were, *how much* more irregular and ineffective your decision-making was in comparison to theirs.

When **evaluating** the success of the MP you should try to make judgements about how the effectiveness of their strokes, breathing, leg-kick helped them be quicker through the water (for instance). You should try to judge the effect of the good technique, the high fitness levels, their understanding of race tactics and how these helped them to win the race.

Exam-style questions

1. Describe a model performance from an activity of your choice. **(4 marks)**

2. Explain the limitations of comparing your own performance to a model performer who is much better than you. **(4 marks)**

3. Evaluate the differences between the model performer's management of emotions and your own in a stressful performance situation. **(4 marks)**

4. Analyse the model performer's ability to make effective decisions within a performance situation. **(4 marks)**

Interpreting qualitative and quantitative, and objective and subjective information

Before we can understand what issues might affect this area we must first understand what the terms mean.

Information is said to be qualitative or quantitative. This in turn affects the degree of objectivity or subjectivity involved in the interpretation of the results.

Qualitative information is information which relates to the quality of a performance. Quantitative information is factual data, statistics, numbers or percentages.

Qualitative information	Quantitative information
How well a winning team played.	The final score.
How successful a tackle was.	The number of successful tackles.
How balanced the turns looked.	The number of half turns in a routine.
How effective the leg kick was.	The time taken to swim a length.
How good the body position was as it went over the bar.	The height cleared in high jump.
How effective the technique was for each clear.	The number of forehand clears played.

- Qualitative information always includes a degree of subjectivity.
- Quantitative information provides more objectivity.
- Subjectivity means opinion, personal feelings and perceptions, which can influence the information gathered.
- Objectivity means information gathered is impartial, fair, unbiased and not influenced by opinions, feelings or perceptions. Therefore it is much more factual.

Mind maps are a good way of presenting the different types of information which can be gathered in a performance.

Here is an example.

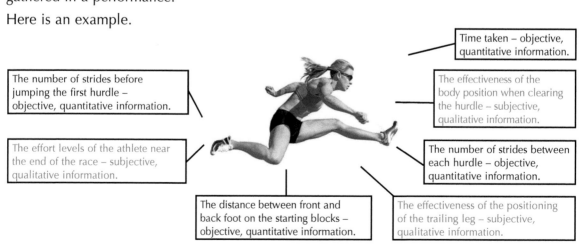

Time taken – objective, quantitative information.

The number of strides before jumping the first hurdle – objective, quantitative information.

The effectiveness of the body position when clearing the hurdle – subjective, qualitative information.

The effort levels of the athlete near the end of the race – subjective, qualitative information.

The number of strides between each hurdle – objective, quantitative information.

The distance between front and back foot on the starting blocks – objective, quantitative information.

The effectiveness of the positioning of the trailing leg – subjective, qualitative information.

Summary

Mental	Emotional
In this area the data generated from these methods tends to be qualitative and subjective. Therefore to make this information as useful as possible (reliable and valid), the conditions under which the methods are administered should be considered carefully. Conclusions drawn from questionnaires, personality inventories and self reflections, for example, should acknowledge that the data is subject to being affected by the time of day, the conditions, the opposition, the context of the performance or any other external influence.	Information about the emotional factor is perhaps likely to be the most subjective and qualitative of all. Care must be taken therefore when drawing conclusions about feelings on their own without considering the environment under which the information was collected. For example, using video footage would confirm triggers or times in a performance when emotions appear affected.

Social	Physical
Checklists can build in an element of quantifiable data collection by including percentages of participants, for example in a local club. Questionnaires used with groups must be clear and understood by all in order that results from within the whole group can be analysed. These results are likely to be qualitative – comments, opinions, feelings which can be grouped together to provide quantifiable evidence of the group's feelings, e.g. '68% of group members felt their views were not listened to'. Team/group feedback has to allow for contributions from all group members. This ensures the views expressed are truly representative of the whole group. Interpretations of the results can then give a clear picture of all important views. Coach feedback should be recorded to ensure important points are noted and not missed 'in the heat of the moment'.	Standardised tests provide quantitative, objective information. This is straightforward to interpret because clear patterns and trends are easy to see and comparisons to norms are possible, e.g. 75 in the Leger Test. Using a method which produces more qualitative information, e.g. GOS, PAR sheets and coach feedback requires attention to be given to reducing the **amount** of opinion involved. This could be done using video to back up or confirm the accuracy of peer/coach assessment. This increases the reliability of the information generated as bias is reduced.

In the exam you might be asked to use your knowledge about the types of information you can collect and to use the skills you have developed to help solve performance problems. You could be asked to:

- **describe** the different types of information which can be gathered when trying to develop performance;
- **explain** which types of information are most useful when planning to develop performance;
- **analyse** the information provided about performance development needs;
- **evaluate** the progress you made from information you collected before and after the performance development process.

When **describing** you must give clear details about the information you gathered, the percentages of successful passes, the numbers of ticks and crosses you counted for each criterion while using a general observation schedule, for example.

When **explaining** the different types of information you collected you must make clear how the different types of information tell you different things and are more or less convincing/relevant/useful/trustworthy when you are going on to improve your performance.

When **analysing** the information you generated you need to look for patterns within the data, similarities or differences, information which was surprising or which confirmed your feelings.

When **evaluating** the progress you made based on the information you collected you need to make the link to the work you completed and the improvements you made. You are required to make a judgement and where possible attribute the improvements demonstrated by your information to the work you carried out.

Exam-style questions

1. Describe the qualitative information you gathered for a factor of your choice. **(4 marks)**

2. Explain how a combination of quantitative and qualitative information gives you a useful picture of performance. **(4 marks)**

3. Analyse the impact of subjective opinions upon a development plan. **(4 marks)**

4. Evaluate the quality of the information you gathered after completing your performance development plan. **(4 marks)**

Receiving/accepting/giving/timing of feedback

Feedback can take many forms when analysing factors which can impact performance.

Here are some examples of score sheets from different activities. These are forms of written feedback.

Blank badminton score sheet

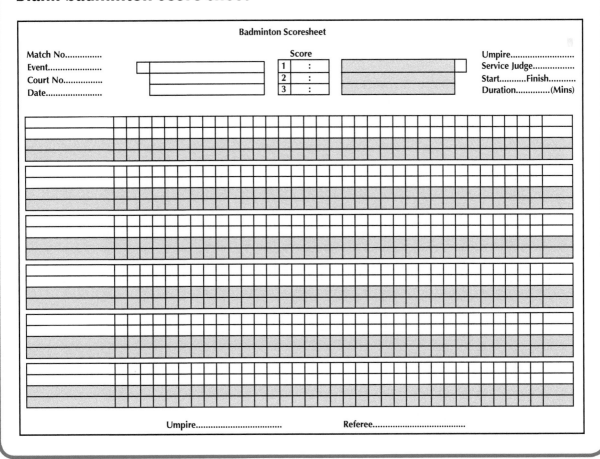

Blank basketball score sheet

OFFICIAL SCORESHEET

Team A: _____ Team B: _____

Competition: _____ Date: _____ Time: _____ Referee: _____

Game No: _____ Place: _____ Umpire: _____ Umpire: _____

Team A:

Time-outs
1st half ☐☐☐
2nd half ☐☐☐
Extra Periods ☐☐

Team fouls
Period 1 | 1 | 2 | 3 | 4 | Period 2 | 1 | 2 | 3 | 4 |
Period 3 | 1 | 2 | 3 | 4 | Period 4 | 1 | 2 | 3 | 4 |

Reg No.	Players	No.	Player in	Fouls 1	2	3	4	5
		4						
		5						
		6						
		7						
		8						
		9						
		10						
		11						
		12						
		13						
		14						
		15						

Coach: _____ Reg No.
Assistant Coach: _____ Reg No.

Team B:

Time-outs
1st half ☐☐☐
2nd half ☐☐☐
Extra Periods ☐☐

Team fouls
Period 1 | 1 | 2 | 3 | 4 | Period 2 | 1 | 2 | 3 | 4 |
Period 3 | 1 | 2 | 3 | 4 | Period 4 | 1 | 2 | 3 | 4 |

Reg No.	Players	No.	Player in	Fouls 1	2	3	4	5
		4						
		5						
		6						
		7						
		8						
		9						
		10						
		11						
		12						
		13						
		14						
		15						

Coach: _____ Reg No.
Assistant Coach: _____ Reg No.

RUNNING SCORE

A	B	A	B	A	B	A	B
1	1	41	41	81	81	121	121
2	2	42	42	82	82	122	122
3	3	43	43	83	83	123	123
4	4	44	44	84	84	124	124
5	5	45	45	85	85	125	125
6	6	46	46	86	86	126	126
7	7	47	47	87	87	127	127
8	8	48	48	88	88	128	128
9	9	49	49	89	89	129	129
10	10	50	50	90	90	130	130
11	11	51	51	91	91	131	131
12	12	52	52	92	92	132	132
13	13	53	53	93	93	133	133
14	14	54	54	94	94	134	134
15	15	55	55	95	95	135	135
16	16	56	56	96	96	136	136
17	17	57	57	97	97	137	137
18	18	58	58	98	98	138	138
19	19	59	59	99	99	139	139
20	20	60	60	100	100	140	140
21	21	61	61	101	101	141	141
22	22	62	62	102	102	142	142
23	23	63	63	103	103	143	143
24	24	64	64	104	104	144	144
25	25	65	65	105	105	145	145
26	26	66	66	106	106	146	146
27	27	67	67	107	107	147	147
28	28	68	68	108	108	148	148
29	29	69	69	109	109	149	149
30	30	70	70	110	110	150	150
31	31	71	71	111	111	151	151
32	32	72	72	112	112	152	152
33	33	73	73	113	113	153	153
34	34	74	74	114	114	154	154
35	35	75	75	115	115	155	155
36	36	76	76	116	116	156	156
37	37	77	77	117	117	157	157
38	38	78	78	118	118	158	158
39	39	79	79	119	119	159	159
40	40	80	80	120	120	160	160

Scores:
Period ① A ___ B ___   ② A ___ B ___
Period ③ A ___ B ___   ④ A ___ B ___
Extra Periods A ___ B ___

Final Score: Team A _____ Team B _____
Name of Winning Team: _____

	Signature	Print Name	
Scorer:	_____	_____	Reg No: _____
Timer:	_____	_____	Reg No: _____
24" operator:	_____	_____	Reg No: _____

Referee: _____ Reg No: _____
Umpire: _____ Reg No: _____
Umpire: _____ Reg No: _____
Captain's signature in case of protest _____

These score sheets give objective feedback about when the games were played, who actually played, how many fouls they picked up, what the eventual score was and even who the officials were.

In terms of being useful for developing performance they would serve only limited purpose as they do not give any real qualitative information about parts of play which were ineffective. A team receiving this feedback

would use this to help analyse player fouls or, in the case of the badminton feedback, to see what the eventual scores were in each of the games. However, it is still helpful when trying to develop performance.

Visual feedback in the form of photographs or recordings is a very useful mechanism to get information on performance. Most performers in most activities would use this type of feedback to help inform future development planning. However, by itself the visual feedback is limited in terms of identification of what should be happening. That is, an observation schedule, checklist or mechanical analysis sheet would be required to allow for comparisons and to check for errors or poor technique.

The analytical possibilities using slow motion, rewind and frame-by-frame controls mean the feedback from the analysis is likely to be accurate and reliable.

Verbal feedback is another means by which feedback can be delivered. A coach, teammate, captain, official, spectator, parent, even an opponent can give verbal feedback on a performance. This could be before, during or after the performance.

Watch the following YouTube clip.

Before you watch it prepare to answer the following questions:

1. How long does the feedback session go on for?

2. Is it clear from the beginning if the team have won or lost the game?

3. What quantity of information is given by head coach Steve Gallon?

4. Do you think the players will remember all the things identified as having been done well?

5. Do you think the players will remember all the things identified as needing attention?

https://www.youtube.com/watch?v=1X8vwrTrkN4

Kinaesthetic feedback is another form of feedback which performers can use to help develop their performance. This feedback becomes useful when the performer knows and can feel he is doing the right thing. This means any written, verbal or visual feedback given as the performer feels he is doing the right thing will confirm the kinaesthetic feedback the performer feels and make it more likely that the correct action is repeated. For example, as the performer hits the shuttle with a straight arm, he feels his technique is exactly right. At the same time the coach gives verbal feedback, saying 'Well done, great technique'. Almost immediately the visual feedback the performer receives is the opponent missing the shuttle and it lands right between the tramlines. Adding together all the different types of feedback means the performer is more likely to try to use the same technique again.

Feedback must be delivered as soon as possible after a performance in order that the performer can link what was done with the associated feedback. So in the example above the badminton player feels the correct technique, the coach confirms it and the visual feedback further confirms this as the shuttle lands where it is supposed to.

Feedback must also be delivered in small chunks to avoid overloading the performer with too much information.

Feedback should contain an element of things which have gone well alongside aspects of performance which require attention. This increases motivation and minimises feelings of negativity a performer might have when given details about too many things which have gone wrong.

Feedback can only be delivered to performers who are ready and willing to listen. The performer must also agree to accept performance feedback. If the feedback is from a source they respect it is more likely that it will be received and used to help improve performance. For example, after a game an opponent telling a performer in the other team that he has to try to time his tackles better isn't going to be well received.

Summary

Mental	Emotional
Feedback about the mental factor must be delivered as soon as possible after the performance finishes. This means the performer is able to reflect accurately on what has just happened. Alternatively, a recorded performance might be shown and paused at times when it was clear that concentration, motivation, levels of arousal or focus drop. Mistakes as a result of poor decision-making may also be viewed retrospectively. Sometimes it might be a challenge to give feedback to a performer, as they might not be in the right frame of mind to receive the information about what was done wrong. In fact the mental factor is still influencing their thinking and behaviour.	Feedback about the emotional factor can in itself be a challenge to deliver because it is often information which is sensitive and may provoke an emotional reaction. Therefore feedback should be delivered when appropriate and by someone who knows the performer. This increases the chances of the performer receiving, accepting and being able to use the feedback provided, e.g. an unknown judge gives a score on a gymnastics sequence. The performer might be disappointed but will probably accept the score. A low score from a judge known and possibly respected by the performer might affect the performer more as they might attach more meaning to this person's criticism.
Social	**Physical**
Care must be taken when giving feedback to a team or group. This is because 'blanket' feedback that is levelled at all team members, regardless of its appropriateness, will not be well-received or accepted by some of the performers. This might be because they feel the feedback is undeserved or not an accurate account of their contributions. Feedback should be 'personalised' where possible so that it can be accepted and used to improve performance further.	Issues related to feedback within this factor tend to be minimal as performers get quite used to being given scores, facts or statistics. However, when this feedback includes a judgement about how good/poor, above/below average the score is, performers sometimes find this difficult to accept.

In the exam you might be asked to:

- **describe** the various types of feedback;
- **explain** how one or more type of feedback helps the performance development process;
- **analyse** the written, verbal, visual or kinaesthetic feedback obtained when developing performance;
- **evaluate** the use of different types of feedback when developing performance.

When **describing** you must give clear details about the different ways feedback can be given.

When **explaining** how a type of feedback helps the performance development process details must be given about what it is that makes a particular type of feedback useful when trying to develop performance.

When **analysing** any of the feedback given, patterns or similarities between the types of feedback must be drawn out.

When **evaluating** the use of different types of feedback you must make a judgement about how they helped you develop your performance.

Exam-style questions

1. Describe two types of feedback **(4 marks)**
2. Analyse the impact of the feedback you received on your level of arousal. **(4 marks)**
3. Evaluate your willingness to receive feedback from another member of your class. **(4 marks)**
4. Explain the importance of timing feedback when developing performance. **(4 marks)**

Purpose of performance development planning

In every walk of life, we should always be trying to improve. For example:

- We should always try to improve our writing skills.
- We should always be trying to improve our counting skills.

These are life skills – skills you will use in many aspects of your life.

The skills we develop in PE are intended to help you develop your performance. The process you go through to do this can also be used in other areas of your life.

Stages

1. Gather data on your whole performance.
2. Identify strengths and development needs.
3. Decide on weaknesses to work on.
4. Plan using knowledge related to performance development.
5. Carry out a planned course of work.
6. Monitor work carried out.
7. Evaluate progress made by going back to Stage 1.

When studying English, you will have:

1. Completed a standardised test.
2. If, for example, reading was identified as a weakness then you will have:
   - agreed targets with teacher;
   - read certain books, completed questions to check understanding;
   - carried out the test again to check for improvements.

By being very clear about what our development needs are, we can be confident in setting about planning to improve them.

Planning always involves:

- forethought – thinking **before** you do something.

This means that you use all of the knowledge you have to organise a course of action *before* you embark on the actual course of action.

This allows you to:

- make sure you have evidence of your development needs;
- set targets which are SMART.

By doing this you will use approaches which will positively impact on your overall performance.

| You would use approaches to improve concentration | Concentration is likely to improve |

Performance development planning will provide the best opportunity for performance to regularly and steadily improve. This is necessary because:

* we need to see improvements as we work through a performance development plan (PDP), as this keeps us motivated;
* improvements to performance indicate that planning has been effective.

'Fail to plan, plan to fail'

Summary

Mental	Emotional
For the mental factor it is necessary to separate features so that the actual development need can be identified and then worked on. Sometimes it is difficult to make clear *which* feature requires attention. For example, lack of concentration can cause poor decision-making and consequently cause a performer to miss cues within the performance context. Therefore, when established, a plan which has observed and checked carefully using appropriate, reliable methods will allow the performer to embark on a path which is designed to gradually improve performance.	To plan to develop the emotional factor it is important to be aware of the different areas which are affected by the different emotions. The plan will set targets which will make clear the approach to be used, the number of sessions and the time and place of the training in order that time is not wasted. Emotions can often be 'trained' during work for other factor areas, therefore time management is effective. For example, while doing a conditioned game for the physical factor to improve the overhead clear, resilience can be developed at the same time by encouraging the performer to keep trying to play the shot – even when it appears to be unsuccessful.

Social	Physical
Within a team or groups, development needs might be relatively varied. Therefore planning must be put in place to make sure the team/group benefits as a whole from any performance development. This allows individual targets to be planned alongside the important team/group targets. Planning will allow the needs of individuals and those of the group to be considered and the training tailored to suit all needs as best as possible.	Planning for the physical factor means that targets are established and a programme of work put in place. This makes sure that the starting levels take into account stages of learning, fitness levels and experience within an activity. By doing this planning the risk of injury is minimised and motivation levels stay quite constant as performers feel able to cope with the demands of training.

In the exam, you might be asked to use your knowledge about performance development planning to outline possible courses of action that a performer might take to begin, continue or restart their training.

You could be asked to:

- **describe** the steps you would go through to begin planning to develop performance;
- **explain** why these steps are necessary;
- **analyse** the success of your planning process;
- **evaluate** whether your planning has been overall effective in bringing about performance improvements.

When **describing** the steps for performance development planning you would make clear what each of the stages in the process were. You would describe collecting data first of all from your 'whole' performance and then describe the process of more focused data for specific aspects of performance.

When **explaining** why each stage was necessary you would be required to give details about why data collection is necessary to provide information which allows you to begin planning to deal with your specific weaknesses.

When **analysing** the success of your planning you would look to give details about how accurate your judgements were about your strengths and weaknesses and the subsequent success of the approaches you decided to use.

An **evaluation** of your overall planning would compare before and after training information relating to performance. If there was an improvement in performance then you could evaluate (measure, judge) that the overall improvements were due to your effective planning.

Exam-style questions

1. Describe a plan for improving a factor of your choice. **(4 marks)**
2. Explain why a plan must be specific to your needs. **(6 marks)**
3. Explain how you could use data to effectively plan for performance development. **(4 marks)**
4. Evaluate how successful your planning was for your exams last year. **(4 marks)**

Prioritising development needs

In any course of action it would be wise to prioritise what needs to be done. For example, when studying for exams you might go through the following process:

- Make a list of the subjects you need to study for.
- Check you have all the materials required for each subject.
- Look at the exam timetable and order your studying to suit when you need to sit the exam.
- Analyse which of the subjects you need to spend most time on, based on how comfortable you feel about what you know and what you still find challenging.
- Draw up a timetable showing which days you will study which subjects.
- Plan for each subject the key areas you need to focus on.
- Organise a jotter, notebook or other device to write, read or draw out any notes you want to take.

There is a certain order in prioritising. It means doing the most important things first. This allows you to have the highest degree of success possible.

For example, if you drew up a timetable *before* checking the exam dates, then it's possible your studying would not help you enough.

In a performance context, you have to prioritise your development needs across the factors. It would be unwise to give all your time and energy to focus on the emotional factor if in fact your physical factor was the area where you needed most improvement.

Therefore the priorities you identify must be based on sound, reliable data collection. This means you are not guessing about what it is that is having the biggest impact on your performance.

Some top performers might be able to give emotional aspects of their performance most of the attention because it could be their lack of self-control that limits their physical fitness, skill level, decision-making and ability to co-operate in a competitive environment.

It would be unlikely that any one factor could be ignored in your own preparation for performance. Therefore complete, all-round preparation requires consideration of all four factors. This might mean you complete a personal development plan (PDP) which has an integrated approach over a period of weeks or months. Or, alternatively, you might focus on one factor for a period of weeks until it has improved to an acceptable level and then give more focus and time to another factor.

For example, once self-control approaches have enabled a badminton player to manage her emotions more effectively, the next priority might be to focus on working with a partner productively in a doubles game of badminton. The techniques or approaches used to help manage self-control would still be used as part of the overall PDP, but would become less of a priority.

Like a pyramid, performance needs are completely dependent on each other. It would be necessary to look at the nature and demands of an activity and then to identify personal development needs which require attention first, i.e. are the priority. A hockey player might identify that before she goes on to develop the speed and agility she requires for her role of striker, she must first establish a good CRE base. This would be her training priority. By focusing on CRE first she will be able to undertake effective speed training to improve her overall performance.

Agility

Speed

CRE

TOP TIP

Examine the nature and demands of an activity when you are trying to find your training priority. This will help you focus on things which are personal but also necessary for the activity which you are performing in.

The place of each of the factors in this pyramid might change as training is done – but they still remain a consideration which requires *some* priority.

Summary

Mental	Emotional
Choosing the most important feature to focus on within the mental factor requires careful consideration of which causes the most negative impact, as the features are so closely linked and dependent on each other. Prioritising the focus for a development plan means working out if lack of concentration is causing a tactic to break down, for example, or if the breakdown of the tactic is because of lack of attention from the performer when the tactic, with everyone's role outlined, was explained.	Since all factors are linked, work done to improve this factor needs decisions to be made about what order work is done in, e.g. if lack of confidence is a problem for a performer then this may be more of a priority than the fact she cannot complete the headspring. It could be that fear (linked to confidence) is the reason why the skill cannot be performed effectively. Therefore analysis of all factors might be worthwhile before a development plan is started. In this way the whole performance needs can be considered.

Social	Physical
Priorities will differ within a team/group or in regard to different genders or cultures. Therefore it is important the issues are clearly defined and agreed amongst all performers within the group. This would mean that progress would be made collectively and an order for factor focus to be established. This in turn means work completed is likely to be more successful.	For the physical factor priorities are usually determined by the role a person is carrying out, the individual strengths and weaknesses or even the time in the season of the performance cycle. For example, in the pre-season for games players a priority is to establish a sound aerobic base upon which all other fitness will be developed. This makes sure more specialised, tailored training can be done as the season commences.
	For skills, the simplest of skills would be the priority for development before those which are more complex. Again, this provides a solid base from which new performance priorities can be selected.
	Establishing simple, effective tactics or compositions would be a focus or priority for a performer. Once these are polished and effective, more complex plays or motifs can be added.

In the exam you might be asked to:
- **describe** your training priority;
- **explain** how you arrived at the conclusion that this was your training priority;
- **analyse** the data which shows this is your priority;
- **evaluate** the reasons for your order of priority.

When **describing** your training priority you must give details about what you can and can't do as a result of this development priority.

When **explaining** how you arrived at the conclusion you must establish why this factor is a priority over all the others.

When **analysing** the data you should try to interpret (use the data to show or illustrate) why this indicates a training priority.

When **evaluating** why you placed one factor as more important than the other you must judge and state the significance of focusing on one factor before you start looking at the others.

Exam-style questions

1. Explain why a sound aerobic base is needed before work begins on other aspects of fitness. **(4 marks)**

2. Describe the difficulties lack of concentration might give a team or group when just one person does not listen. **(4 marks)**

3. Identify the type of development plan which has more than one factor as its focus. **(1 mark)**

4. Explain why training priorities must be based on information collected. **(4 marks)**

Potential impacts of factors on performance development

You should know about the four factors affecting performance.

You also need to consider their impact when you are trying to develop your performance.

- The physical factor is split into fitness, skills and structures and strategies or composition.
- The mental factor is concerned with all thinking and cognitive processes.
- The emotional factor is about your feelings.
- The social factor is about dealing with working on your own, with or against others.

Physical factors can affect your ability to carry out a personal development plan. If your fitness is lacking, then any work you carry out can be affected.

For example, if you had poor cardio-respiratory endurance (CRE) and you were working to improve it using conditioning drills, the level of skill you had would need to be taken into account when planning your circuit. That is, if your dribbling was also poor, it is possible you wouldn't be able to get your heart rate (HR) high enough dribbling, because you could only dribble slowly in order to keep control of the ball.

Similarly, if your CRE was poor, using repetition drills in badminton for 10 minutes non-stop might impact on the quality of return you could make because you were out of breath.

The **social factor** can impact on your work during performance development because you might need to work co-operatively with someone to complete passive stretching exercises. If this was something you had no experience of, then it's likely you would have difficulty carrying out the role required of you.

In gymnastics, if you needed a 'spotter' to help you develop your somersault, you would need to make sure the 'spotter' was knowledgeable and skilled enough to carry out the role effectively and safely.

Having a feeder/passive defender/supporter/peer observer requires you to:

- make sure they know what to do;
- make sure they have the skills for the job.

How you feel (the **emotional factor**) can have an impact on how motivated, committed and determined you are to carry out your development plan. If you are happy, sad or angry, the work you complete might be less than intended because of the way you feel.

If your concentration and decision-making are poor (**mental factor**), then the quality of work you carry out will probably drop. This means you won't make the progress you should expect and then a vicious circle might occur, where you concentrate more on what is going wrong than on what you should be doing.

The knowledge you have about what the different factors are and how they impact on performance should help you in this area of the course. You need to be able to apply this knowledge when working on developmental performance.

Therefore:

- If fitness is a problem while trying to develop skills, keep the drills short, give lots of rest to allow recovery and make sure the quality of skill is not affected by poor fitness levels.

- In conditioning drills for CRE, make sure the skills you choose to develop are ones which allow you to do them at pace so that your HR can be pushed into its training zone.

- When needing a person to work alongside you to help develop performance, choose someone you know has the skills and knowledge to carry out *their* role in order to help you fix *your* weakness.

- Try to 'set aside' your feelings when working to develop your performance. Use some of the techniques to manage emotion before and during your training (such as positive self-talk) to focus on the training you need to do and not the way you feel.

TOP TIP

You can use the approaches already used in PDPs to help you manage your performance development process.

Summary

Mental	Emotional
The mental factor can influence the outcome of the performance development process. Lack of concentration can mean approaches are not carried out effectively. This would mean performance would not be as positively impacted as possible, i.e. the training wouldn't have the desired outcome. Working to improve decision-making or problem-solving with low levels of motivation or levels of arousal might mean a performer would give up when the work became more challenging.	If a performer does not feel ready to train, then it's likely the work carried out will be ineffective. If pessimism is a strong influence for a performer then they will not feel as though training can make a difference. This will obviously affect the quality and quantity of training done.

Social	Physical
Group dynamics can have an impact on the effort levels present when training or developing performance. Peer influence can also affect the involvement and motivation a performer contributes. This would mean relationships within the group could break down and cause further problems.	If a performer is not physically able to carry out work to develop performance then it is likely that performance itself will not improve. For example, using a conditioned game to improve a weak overhead clear demands a certain amount of stamina to be able to keep moving around the court. If this is not present then the tiredness and fatigue are the reasons the conditioned game was not effective – not a poor overhead clear.

In the exam you might be asked to:

- **describe** the impact of a factor on your performance development;
- **explain** the course of action you might use to minimise the effects of the decision factor on performance development;
- **analyse** the improvements you make to performance development as a result of a course of action you've taken;
- **evaluate** the success of your training before you dealt with the impact of any factor and after you dealt with it.

When **describing** how your performance is affected you must give details about what things went wrong, what things you were able or unable to do and how the factor affected the success of your overall performance.

When **explaining** the potential impact of these factors you must be clear about why this factor can make things go wrong or stop you being able to carry out your performance effectively.

When **analysing** the impact of these factors you should try to quantify how many mistakes were made, for example, or how often you felt unable to carry out the performance effectively.

When **evaluating** the effects of the factors on performance a judgement has to be made about **how** influential the factors were in helping or hindering the overall success of the performance.

Exam-style questions

1. Explain how the mental factor might affect your performance development plan process. **(4 marks)**

2. Describe the challenges the social factor might have on performance development. **(4 marks)**

3. Explain how you could use positive self-talk to help you get into the right frame of mind to complete a session of your performance development plan. **(4 marks)**

4. Explain what evidence you might gather to show you are managing the impact of the four factors on performance. **(4 marks)**

Performance development goals

Goal-setting has proved to be an effective way of increasing focus when developing performance.

Setting goals can only help in the performance development process if they are:
- Specific – clearly stating 'I want to be able to ...'
- Measurable – have some quantitative or qualitative data to assess progress.
- Achievable – be realistic from the starting point to the intended target.
- Relevant – suit the needs of the individual and activity.
- Time set – have timescales associated with them.

Goals can be split into three main categories:
- Outcome goals – to win – dependent on who you are competing against.
- Performance goals – to improve only your own performance.
- Process goals – to improve aspects of performance, mechanical execution of skills.

All three types of goals have a part to play when developing performance.
- Outcome goal – to win today's match.
- Performance goal – can be used to check progress towards achieving process goals.
- Process goal – can be used to help you achieve an outcome goal.

An example:

Outcome goal – to win each race. Tend to be long-term but are affected by opposition.

Process goal – run 5-minute mile pace.

Performance goal – to complete the race in less than 4 hours, largely focuses on how the individual performs.

Different activities will require different types of goals to be set. Goals are also dependent on individual needs, team/group needs or even the time and season.

An outcome goal requires associated process and performance goals. That is, to win, you must have a plan (goal) which establishes the process goals (the techniques and strategies) required to perform effectively within the actual performance and the performance goals which 'set the standard' for the overall performance.

Summary

Mental	Emotional
Mental development plans require clear goals. This will allow the focus to be on specific areas for improvement. The goals may be short term – to reduce the effects of poor focus of attention by using positive self-talk words or long term, to improve concentration by training to make use of imagery to shut out distractions before focus is lost.	Goals for the development of features within the emotional factor will be very personal and can be very long term. The goals need to take account of the fact that emotions are affected by many external and sometimes genetic or historical influences. These things are difficult to control and behaviour as a result of these emotions has probably been established for a long time. However, small changes and long-term goals can most certainly bring about positive changes in a person's emotional characteristics.

Social	Physical
Goals which are shared within a team/group need to be revisited regularly. This is because an individual can 'hide' in a group and can (deliberately or otherwise) damage the group's chances of achieving their goals. For example, someone who does not see or agree that there is a lack of communication in the group might not enter into training with the right attitude and, as a consequence, is unlikely to try the same approaches within the performance setting.	Goals for this factor can be planned quite straightforwardly. An increase in the number of successful high serves, shuttles completed in the Leger Test or the percentage of successful fast breaks are quite easily evaluated. Goals can then be reset to ensure performance development is assured.

In the exam you might be asked to use your knowledge about performance development goals and how they are used. You could be asked to:

- **describe** a performance goal;
- **explain** why you require to set goals with a performance development programme;
- **analyse** how effective goal-setting has helped you achieve success in performance development;
- **evaluate** the success you achieved for the goal you set.

When **describing** a performance goal you must provide details of exactly what it is you intend focusing on.

When **explaining** the goal you would be expected to say why this goal would help improve your overall performance.

When **analysing** the process of goal setting you would need to show the value of goal setting to performance improvement at each stage of your PDP.

When **evaluating** the success or otherwise of your goal you would need to show that by having a goal it made you more focused and that without it you might not have made as much progress. Reflect on the improvement shown in your data to support any judgements you make.

Exam-style questions

1. Describe two goals you have set. **(2 marks)**
2. Explain why these goals are relevant to you. **(4 marks)**
3. Explain why we need a variety of goals when we are working to develop performance. **(4 marks)**
4. Analyse improvements in performance in relation to the goals you set yourself. **(4 marks)**
5. Describe the three types of goals. **(3 marks)**

Approaches to meet performance development goals

The approaches used must enable you to achieve your goals. The organisation of the approaches as part of your performance development plan must allow you to make steady progress towards your aim. Therefore, the following must be clearly identified:

- Type of skill you are trying to develop.
- Aspect of fitness you are trying to improve.
- Tactic or strategy you are focusing on.
- Particular area of the social factor which requires attention.
- Main emotion which is having an impact on performance.
- Area within the mental factor which needs focus.

By being specific about what it is you are going to work on, the most suitable approach can be identified.

The approach should allow you to experience execution of the development need in as similar a 'context' as possible to the live performance situation. In this way, transference of development need is most likely.

For example:

Physical factor – fitness
- Development need – cardio respiratory endurance.
- Activity – hockey.
- Approach to be used – Fartlek training.
- Suitability of this approach – the approach utilises the same types/paces of running as those required in a game.

Social factor – team dynamics

- Development need – more positive relationships between group members required.
- Activity – dance.
- Approach to be used – group work.
- Suitability of this approach – the approach breaks down barriers between individuals, addresses misunderstandings and enables more positive, healthy and productive relationships to be established.

Mental factor – mental toughness

- Development need – trying to stay positive throughout an entire match.
- Activity – tennis.
- Approach to be used – positive self-talk.
- Suitability of this approach – this can be learnt in training and then used in a live performance context quite easily as it becomes part of a thinking process when things go wrong or even when they go well.

Emotional factor – fear – decision-making

- Development need – following a mistake, a performer begins to hesitate when taking a shot.
- Activity – basketball.
- Approach to be used – visualisation.
- Suitability of this approach – when the player steps up to take a free throw, he/she can pause and momentarily picture/visualise him/herself scoring the basket.

Thinking about the development need and how it should be carried out in the live performance situation makes sure you use an approach which is *specific* to that area. By doing this you will have the greatest chance of success.

Specificity requires consideration of the:

- type of skill, aspect of fitness or emotion being developed;
- conditions under which the development need has to be used;
- stage of learning of the performer;
- experience of the performer.

Using an approach to meet development goals which is specific to all of these areas, makes sure that the approach allows the performer practical exposure of how the skill aspect of fitness or emotion is required in the live performance context. This means that when it is required in this situation, the performer already has experience of using the approach in the same type of conditions, or has practised or trained using an approach which allows development of skills, techniques or qualities required for the real performance.

Summary

Mental	Emotional
The chosen approach to develop this factor has to be specific to the performer, their role, their experience and the activity. For example, concentration can differ depending on how tight a match is or what position a player is carrying out. Therefore the approach used must take into account the conditions under which the mental features are to be used. In this way training will be very specific to develop these areas to be used in the required context, e.g. there would be little point in carrying out a decision-making drill for a zone defence with no offensive players. Decisions need to be made *while* the ball is being passed around – just as in the live performance situation.	Approaches need to match the area of development otherwise it could be that training could be counterproductive to another factor. For example, if training is done to develop self-belief and it takes no account of the performer's place within a group then an over-confident, self-assured person could cause chaos to dynamics. Therefore the feature, which is the focus, needs to ensure that the performer sees how self-belief needs to be managed when working alongside other people. Training would need to be specific to develop self-belief to enhance overall performance, i.e. take account of other people's feelings.
Social	**Physical**
Within this factor a range of social 'issues' may affect performance development. Therefore a group or team could have different specific processes they carry out as part of performance development. The overall goal for a team or group should remain the same for all members and the approaches used must allow the areas of development to be the focus.	Approaches must be designed to have a positive impact on the goals set. This will be assured by matching the needs to the best course of action. Taking into account fitness levels, stages of learning and previous experience will ensure the training begins at the right place and motivation and engagement levels remain high throughout the programme.

In the exam you might be asked to:

- **describe** an approach which you chose to help you achieve a performance development goal;
- **explain** why this approach is appropriate;
- **analyse** how this specific approach is successful in helping you to improve a development need;
- **evaluate** the success you experienced in a live performance following your personal development plan.

When **describing** the approach you must outline its most important qualities and make clear how it is carried out.

When **explaining** the appropriateness of the approach you must link its important qualities to the areas which require attention in your performance. That is, what is it that makes this approach suitable for this particular factor?

When **analysing** the success of the approach used you would be expected to make clear the improvements in the factor within performance. You could also write about improvements shown in the data collected from tests, or observations outwith the actual performance, to show how the approach had helped you improve a development need.

When **evaluating** the success experienced in a live performance judgements would need to be made and backed up by data about how much better your performance was after the performance development process as a result of the approach you used.

Exam-style questions

1. Describe one approach you used within a personal development plan. **(2 marks)**

2. Explain the need for specificity when choosing an approach to develop performance. **(4 marks)**

3. Analyse two approaches you have used within a personal development plan. **(4 marks)**

4. Explain how you would evaluate the effectiveness of one of your chosen approaches. **(4 marks)**

Purpose and value of recording, monitoring and evaluating performance development

Performance development **is** actually a **process**. That means action is taken over a series of interdependent steps towards an end.

Performance development should be based on reflections of what has been done and considerations about what must be done next. These reflections need to be written down – **recorded**.

The record of performance development, in whatever format you choose, then becomes a resource to be used as part of the monitoring and evaluation process.

This means judgements about what your next steps should be can be based on evidence of work completed.

Each step in performance development should be recorded. This allows you to **monitor** the work you are completing. Information about what you did, how long you did it for, when you did it, where you did it and how you felt are all pieces of important information which will inform each step of the PDP.

Monitoring as you go along allows you to see clearly:

- what you did last;
- what you should do next;
- the progress you are making;
- how to stay motivated and focused.

Monitoring needs to be:

- regular – done after each work session;
- systematic – recorded logically in an organised way.

Regular and systematic monitoring allows you to:

- take appropriate action on the next session;
- be confident that changes and adaptations to development plan sessions are based on judgements about work already done and not opinions or assumptions about what you *might* do next.

The purpose of **evaluating** performance development relates to judgements you make after you complete a programme of work. At this stage you might complete your recording method by giving an overall summary about how effective your overall PDP was in developing your performance.

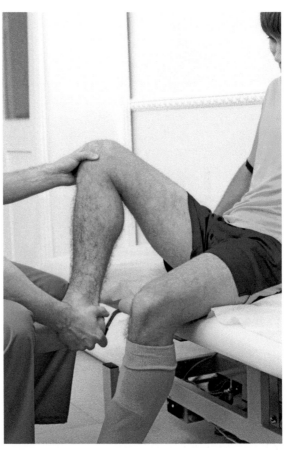

The judgements you make will then help you plan for the future. This plan will include judgements about the effectiveness of the approaches you used. If you found the approaches easy to use, interesting and motivating, it is likely you would consider using them again. However, if you struggled to make progress, or found the approaches too challenging or boring, you might decide to exclude them from future performance development planning.

Judging the evidence you have *recorded* as part of your monitoring over a number of sessions may allow you to see errors in your planning. For example, if you decided to increase your training and then experienced an injury, it might be possible to evaluate that you tried to do too much too soon.

Evaluation of work completed is vital if performance development is to be a worthwhile and safe process.

TOP TIP

The methods you use for monitoring performance can also be used to keep a record of the work you carry out, e.g. a training diary can be used throughout a training programme to monitor progress in each whole game over a season. The same diary can be used before training and then again at the end of the personal development plan to evaluate overall progress made.

Summary

Mental	Emotional
Keeping a diary throughout personal development in which a performer records the types of decisions made and their outcomes will help her to monitor whether there is any progress in a particular area.	Keeping a note of how the performer feels after training within a personal reflection profile will allow the performer to monitor when exactly they feel they may lose control of their emotions. This personal reflection will allow the performer to make meaningful changes or adaptations to the programme so that they can come up with a solution. After training, the performer would be able to look back over the profile and make a subjective judgement as to how their performance has improved or changed.
Social	**Physical**
A coach taking notes will allow the team to see a record detailing exactly what worked well for the team and what did not and then apply solutions. If a team feels at the end of training that they work better together and can see the positive outcomes from the coach's feedback, it will allow the team to channel more energy into working as one unit.	During the monitoring process a performer will note all times or results – this quantitative data will help them to make comparisons. This record should be completed regularly and using the same protocol used for prior data collection. For example, the performance context would need to be the same. This way the performer will have an accurate record throughout the monitoring process. The monitoring process will allow the performer to make progress checks against set targets. This will help them stay motivated throughout their training. This process will also lead to a final evaluation, where the performer will be able to determine the impact of training on performance. This will allow the performer to consider the next steps for their physical performance.

In the exam you might be asked to:

- **describe** how you monitored performance development;
- **explain** how you evaluated performance development;
- **analyse** monitoring methods;
- **evaluate** a programme of work completed as part of a PDP.

When **describing** the process you went through to monitor performance development you need to provide details about where information was stored, what format it was in, how often it was completed and by whom.

When **explaining** how you evaluated performance development you would need to say how you checked for improvements at the end of the performance development process and why you carried it out this way.

When **analysing** the methods you used to check for ongoing progress you would comment on or compare how useful particular methods were at keeping information together and how successful they were at generating usable and easy to interpret information.

When **evaluating** a programme of work you have to make clear if the programme had the intended outcome and perhaps comment on your recommendations for using this approach again.

Exam-style questions

1. Describe one method used to monitor performance development. **(4 marks)**

2. Compare the work you completed at the beginning of your personal development plan to that at the end of the plan. **(4 marks)**

3. Analyse the evidence your monitoring methods generated which indicated it was necessary to change or adapt your personal development plan. **(4 marks)**

4. Evaluate the progress you made on completion of your development plan. **(4 marks)**

Key planning information

The information in a performance development plan is dependent on the:

- nature of the activity;
- demands of the activity;
- ability of the performer;
- experience of the performer.

The planning information allows you to:

- set appropriate short-term goals;
- set appropriate long-term goals;
- identify appropriate approaches to be used;
- organise necessary resources for the PDP.

By knowing what the nature of your activity is, you can then use the planning information to include approaches which will be appropriate within your PDP.

The process would be to:

1. Establish your starting point. This might be:
   - current level of fitness;
   - current stage of learning;
   - relevant statistics indicating impact of factor on performance.
2. Establish your long-term goal – what do you want performance to be like after a season, competition or event?
3. Identify and decide on outcome, performance and process goals which will help you achieve your chosen outcome.
4. Research, try out and agree the most appropriate approaches to be used within your PDP.

Summary

Mental	Emotional
Some activities require an increased level of concentration at specific points in the performance, e.g. when taking free throws in basketball. The performer may want to apply specific targets for improving their concentration during this period and then work on approaches to develop this area.	Being able to consider the emotional requirements of a performer takes time and experience. The performer needs to make sure they carry out a period of self-reflection, where they highlight the key areas for emotional development. This will allow the performer to set a clear target for improvement and then develop appropriate approaches to use. This target may be as simple as using positive statements throughout training and performance.
Social	**Physical**
For example, during a team performance, a team could set a target to improve overall communication. This may have been acknowledged as an area of weakness in previous performances. Having a specific target for the whole team to work towards can encourage the team to improve through working together.	For a fitness personal development programme, it is essential to set short- and long-term targets, which are specific, measurable, achievable, realistic and can be completed within the time set out. For example, in an agility programme it's important that the performer has knowledge of the level of agility they already have before then considering the agility requirements they need to develop. They will need to review their levels of agility throughout training so that they know the targets set are achievable and realistic.

In the exam you might be asked to:

- **describe** one piece of key planning information;
- **explain** why planning is required for performance development;
- **analyse** the usefulness of your planning information;
- **evaluate** the progress you made based on the planning information you gathered.

To **describe** the key planning information you need to give details about the data which had most influence on your planning for performance development.

When **explaining** why planning is necessary you would need to link all of the areas for development with your reduced effectiveness within the performance. This would need to make clear that by being prepared to work on these areas your intention was to make your overall performance better.

When **analysing** the usefulness of this information you need to take each piece of planning information and show how it highlights the problems you have in your overall performance.

When **evaluating** progress you must make judgements about how successful you have been in bringing about changes to your overall performance based on your initial plans.

Exam-style questions

1. Describe the most important piece of planning information you used. **(4 marks)**

2. Explain the planning information you made use of to organise your PDP. **(4 marks)**

3. Analyse the use of goal-setting within planning for performance development. **(4 marks)**

4. Evaluate the accuracy of your key planning information. **(4 marks)**

Recording and monitoring methods or tools

If performance development is to be effective, it is important to record the following:

- progress made;
- approaches used;
- next steps.

A careful note of development needs and approaches used to improve these needs, along with reflections from the performer, will establish an accurate 'database'. The information stored in the 'database' can indicate progress achieved and changes or alterations made to the personal development plan.

This information can be stored in the following ways for the four factors:

- training diary;
- personal reflections journal;
- questionnaires;
- disciplinary record;
- coach feedback records;
- standardised fitness test scores/results;
- league table results;
- ranking or classification systems for players/dancers/gymnasts.

By keeping accurate records:

- new development needs can be identified;
- progress towards targets can be made clear;
- motivation levels are more likely to remain high;
- evidence can be accumulated which can substantiate (prove) whether a course of action has been beneficial or otherwise.

Data recorded can be quantitative or qualitative. Quantifiable data is percentage shots in court, the number of successful tackles/passes/interceptions – in other words, numbers. Qualitative data is information about what the performance looked like, opinions and observations, and overall summaries of the effectiveness of skills, techniques, tactics etc. Quantifiable data is objective (factual) and qualitative data is subjective (opinion). Records should be a combination of both types of data where possible. This means there is an all-round accurate, detailed picture of performance.

Summary

Mental, e.g.	Emotional, e.g.
A training diary can be kept throughout the PDP to take notes of how specific approaches to develop decision-making are working. This means the performer will be able to monitor whether progress has been made to agreed targets. After each training session, notes about what decisions were made and the impact of these decisions will be taken.	Keeping a personal reflection on how the performer feels their PDP is going will allow for subjective opinions to be made. The qualitative data will give opinions, views and observations on the PDP. After training, the performer would be able to look back over the profile and make a subjective judgement as to how their performance has improved or changed.
Social, e.g.	**Physical, e.g.**
During a team performance it may be that a team target has been set to improve overall team communication. Making comparisons between communication questionnaires will allow the team to look back and see whether there has been any progress made.	Quantitative data, which can be collected throughout the PDP, whether through fitness tests, skills test or observation schedules, allows the performer to have factual information on how well their PDP is progressing. This can be a valid tool, alongside subjective opinions, to give an accurate picture of the impact of the PDP.

In the exam you might be asked to:

- **describe** a recording method which could be used to gather data on a factor's impact on performance;
- **explain** how appropriate this method is to record progress;
- **analyse** the features of the recording method to enable you to keep accurate records;
- **evaluate** the contribution this recording method made to the overall performance development process.

When **describing** you must give clear details about what methods can be used to keep a note of the work that is being done. This should include details about what facility each method gives you to store information.

When **explaining** the appropriateness of the method you have to make clear how this helps you keep an accurate check on what is done, how you feel and what your next steps will be.

When **analysing** the different features of the method you need to make clear how the different columns allow you to keep a methodical note of the progress you are making, allowing you to make decisions about what you need to do next. You need to analyse the different parts of the method to show you know what each part allows you to do.

When **evaluating** the contribution the method makes to your PDP process you should highlight the benefits and limitations of the method and then make an overall judgement of whether the method has allowed you to take steady, planned steps through your training due to the methodical recording of information.

Exam-style questions

1. Describe a method to monitor the impact of a Social factor. **(4 marks)**
2. Explain the importance of monitoring your personal development programme. **(4 marks)**
3. Analyse the effectiveness of the method selected. **(4 marks)**

Production and implementation of performance development plans

In this area of the mandatory knowledge and skills you will use all of the information you have learnt to put together a plan which will work on your development needs. You will then have to implement the plan, carrying it out over a period of time. This should include:

- SMART targets set according to the needs identified and the nature, demands and context of the activity. Example of target: I want to mark my opponent for the whole match. These targets are required to give focus to the work you carry out and to ensure that progress is safe and gradual.

- Details of the frequency, duration and make-up of the sessions. This provides structure to the work you carry out and makes sure you progress training where required or develop approaches to ensure improvements are continuous.

- Information related to how the programme will be structured – principles of training for fitness, principles of effective practice for skills, principles of play for tactics/ strategies. Plans for the social, mental or emotional factors can also be progressed by reducing time to make decisions within a training programme or using self-talk less during a plan to improve confidence.

- Details of how and when progress will be monitored and recorded. This should show that the results or success of work undertaken influences when training is changed or adapted.

- Feedback received from peers or teachers/coaches. A performance development plan will change as feedback is received about how performance is developing.

- Evidence of how the PDP has changed or adapted as the process goes on. This evidence will always be aiming to show if performance is being positively affected by the approaches used.

- Reflections about what needs to be done next based on evaluations of the work completed. Looking back at work that has been completed and also checking the progress/impact on performance can identify new development needs.

Summary

Mental	Emotional
The performer should set SMART targets before setting out to design their PDP. The target may be as simple as improving concentration during a specific part of the performance. Details of the approaches to be used – such as mental rehearsal – should be built into the programme, with consideration of the frequency and duration. The performer may want to use a diary to monitor their PDP so that they can make changes and adaptations to the PDP as they go along. A final evaluation of their concentration after the PDP has been completed would help them consider what needs to be done next.	The performer should set SMART targets before setting out to design their PDP. The target may be as simple as controlling their anger during the performance. Details of the approaches to be used – such as visualisation – should be built into the programme, and when and how these will be carried out. The performer may receive feedback from their teammates or coach during their PDP, which would help to monitor the impact anger is having on their performance, and progress of the plan.

Social	Physical
The performer should set SMART targets before designing their PDP. The target may be as simple as improving communication skills during the PDP. Details of the approaches to be used – such as communication drills – should be built into the programme, with consideration of the frequency and duration of these drills. The performer may want to use a diary to monitor their PDP so that they can make changes and adaptations to the PDP as they go along.	The performer should set SMART targets before setting out to design their PDP. The following should be applied depending on the type of PDP: 1. the principles of training for a fitness PDP; 2. principles of effective practice for skills training; 3. principles of play for tactics/strategies; 4. choreographic devices for compositional performances. Details of the approaches to be used – such as interval training, gradual build-up, tactical drills, technique repetition – should be developed, depending on the physical factor being explored. Using different quantitative monitoring methods, such as fitness testing and observation schedules, can be carried out throughout training so that comparisons can be made.

In the exam you might be asked to:

- **describe** the steps you went through to organise your PDP;
- **explain** why you might organise your PDP the way you did;
- **analyse** the usefulness of the approaches contained in the PDP;
- **evaluate** the progress you made from the beginning to the end of your PDP.

When **describing** you must take each step and describe what you did at each point.

When **explaining** you should say why you included the approaches you did.

When **analysing** the approaches you should take each one and compare the benefits or limitations of each in helping you improve your performance.

When **evaluating** you need to use evidence from data collection to back up judgements about the progress you have made.

Exam-style questions

1. Describe SMART targets that could be set to develop the Physical factor. **(4 marks)**
2. Explain why these targets are SMART. **(4 marks)**
3. What principles do you need to consider to develop a fitness PDP? **(4 marks)**
4. Describe methods of monitoring the PDP. **(4 marks)**
5. Compare pre- and post-PDP evaluations of your performance. **(4 marks)**

Adapting performance development plans

A development plan, by its very nature, must change as you carry it out. This ensures:

* performer continually improves;
* motivation levels remain high.

Depending on the factor and associated approaches being used, changes and adaptations will vary.

When working on fitness within the physical factor, the principles of training should be applied. In order for fitness levels to steadily increase, as the body adapts to each training load the following will need to change:

* frequency;
* intensity;
* duration.

As skill-development progresses, more challenging practices will be required as the performer moves from the cognitive stage of learning to the associative, and eventually to the autonomous stage. This will allow the performer to develop step by step.

If a tactic is the focus of development, then use drills which take the individual or team through a process of:

* understanding roles and responsibilities within the tactic;
* using the tactic with no defender or with a co-operative opponent;
* moving to a passive or less co-operative opponent;
* moving to an active or fully competitive opponent.

The approaches used for the mental or emotional factors often do not obey the same 'rules' for progression. Rather, when using these approaches, the length of time can be reduced. For example, a performer who uses:

* visualisation;
* deep breathing;
* imagery;
* positive self-talk;
* mental rehearsal

might find that as their concentration, decision-making, confidence, mental toughness, self-control improves, the need to use the approach reduces. This might be because the anxiety, stress or emotion that was causing the problem is now under control. In this PDP, the frequency of use of these approaches might reduce over a period of months.

This would be shown in recorded/monitoring methods.

Also, within the social factor, plans adapt as:

- team or group dynamics improve;
- roles are agreed and understood;
- individual or group members' self-esteem increases;
- communication strategies are used effectively.

As the plans are adapted, progress is continually improved.

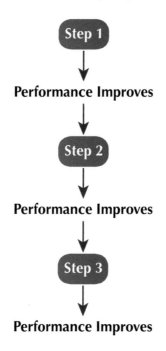

Step 1

↓

Performance Improves

↓

Step 2

↓

Performance Improves

↓

Step 3

↓

Performance Improves

Sometimes plans have to be adapted because progress is not being made.

This might be because:

- the 'steps' are too big or challenging;
- of injury;
- of absence from training;
- of boredom.

In this case, the plan would need to be adapted – going *back* a step to re-establish training at a level appropriate for a performer returning after injury or absence. If the cause of lack of progress is because of boredom, then more variety should be built in to the adapted development plan.

Summary

Mental	Emotional
If levels of concentration do not improve, the performer will need to go back and re-think the approaches. For example, setting cues during training may help the performer, rather than the phases of mental rehearsal.	Throughout a PDP for developing ways of dealing with anxiety, the performer will need to adapt training depending on the situation. Changing the approach to control anxiety may be as simple as having a teammate's reassurance or taking themselves through positive self-talk. Both can have a positive impact depending on the situation.
Social	**Physical**
When a PDP has been designed to improve team work, the effect of these approaches can increase a team's desire to work together and improve together. As the training progresses, scenarios can be built in to add even more challenge into team situations, where the team must emphasise working together to overcome these challenges.	Adapting a Physical PDP is important to overcome any issues with boredom and lack of variety. It may be as simple as adding a new skill-related drill that has not been completed before to raise the performer's interest.

In the exam you might be asked to:

- **describe** the changes you made to your PDP;
- **explain** why these changes were necessary;
- **analyse** the indicators which told you to adapt your PDP;
- **evaluate** the impact of the changes to your PDP.

When **describing** the changes make sure to give details of all of the steps you went through as you carried out the plan.

When **explaining** why the changes were necessary you must link the change to a reason for progressing the plan. Often the change is needed to keep motivation levels high or to make sure there is a continual improvement.

When **analysing** the indicators that tell you it's time to adapt the plan you should include information about how much motivation levels dropped, how progress was reduced.

When **evaluating** the impact of these changes you should be able to judge the success of changing your plan as your progress improved, how your motivation levels increased and how performance overall was positively impacted.

Exam-style questions

1. Describe two ways you adapted your PDP. **(4 marks)**
2. Explain which of the two adaptations was most challenging. **(4 marks)**
3. Analyse the effect of the changes to your PDP on your level of motivation. **(4 marks)**
4. Evaluate the success of the changes you made to your PDP. **(4 marks)**

Future performance development planning

Future performance development planning should be an ongoing process. It is unlikely that a performer would complete a PDP and stop working on, or completely forget about, the area they had initially planned to develop.

Rather, future needs are centred around:

- making progress in overcoming a development need;
- finding a new area of development need.

The development need may still require attention, but becomes less of a *priority*.

In this way, a new, more pressing 'feature' becomes the focus for performance development.

This would require the PDP to keep the original development need 'ticking over' – still gradually improving – even if only by a small percentage each week.

Any future development needs need to be justified by a performance evaluation. In this way, the pre-planning requirements discussed earlier are given serious consideration. That is:

- Have I improved in the area I was working on?
- What must I do to make sure this improvement is not compromised, i.e. if I stop working on it, will my performance deteriorate? Or, what must I now do to maintain the level achieved?

The next decision about future performance development planning involves a systematic review and evaluation of:

- improvements made at the end of a PDP;
- targets achieved at the end of a PDP;
- new/current performance development needs;
- the approaches used within the PDP.

TOP TIP

Many performers continue to develop their overall performance throughout a PDP. This allows them to set new targets and goals according to the demands of their activity.

Summary

Mental	Emotional
Planning for the mental factor will be an ongoing process depending on the performance challenge. A high-profile event may require extra levels of motivation and the drive to put in extra training to achieve success. This may require extra time for training and to maintain motivation, the performer may therefore need to have a clear sense of achievement after only a short period of time.	If a performer has a specific challenge, e.g. controlling their anger, it will be important that this is always considered in their future development. This may require particular situations being set up to challenge the performer, so that they can use specific approaches to overcome these challenges.

Social	Physical
Occasionally the PDP will not go to plan and the performance may plateau or even deteriorate. For example, when a team is using different approaches for group dynamics, it may become apparent that not all performers have the positive mind-set needed for improvement. At this stage, future development needs would need to be changed to incorporate a more positive outcome.	As training continues, a performer may wish to focus less on their aerobic endurance and more on the tactical and compositional elements of their performance. This requires the performer to keep aerobic approaches in their PDP, but add in the roles they need to carry out in their performance.

In the exam you might be asked to:

- **describe** your future development needs;
- **explain** how a new PDP might be organised;
- **analyse** the new development needs;
- **evaluate** your performance on completion of your performance development plan.

A **description** of future development needs would make clear areas of performance that are now to be the focus of development. Details describing what happens during performance should be given for each of the development needs.

An **explanation** about the future plan should link what is going to be done with the specific reasons for doing it this way.

To **analyse** the new needs, data would be used to confirm that development needs have been chosen correctly. You need to be clear about how much of a problem the new areas are.

To **evaluate** you should compare the data from pre-development plans and post-development plans. A judgement should then be made to confirm if the plan has brought about positive changes in performance.

Exam-style questions

1. Compare your pre- and post-training performances. **(4 marks)**
2. Explain why you have prioritised your future development need. **(4 marks)**
3. Analyse the impact of this 'new' development need on your performance. **(4 marks)**

The scenario question

This area of the exam will require you to bring the skills, knowledge and understanding you have developed through both units:

- factors impacting performance;
- performance skills.

The question will begin by providing a 'prompt'.

This 'prompt' could be:

- text – a written diagram of a performance problem;
- a graph – information which you may have to interpret to help identify a performance problem;
- a table – again, information/data, which you will be required to interpret or analyse to help you deal with the performance problem.

Activity date	Number of instances of poor self control
3/6/2014	||||| ||||| ||

Each year you will be given one factor to write about, and be able to choose one more factor of your choice to help you answer the questions.

The 'given' factor will be the factor *not* covered in the questions in the first part of the exam.

The scenario is worth 16 marks.

You should set aside at least *30 minutes* to complete this.

Whichever format (graph, text or table) is used to present the scenario, the procedure for tackling it should be the same:

1. Identify the *named* factor.
2. Establish whether the scenario relates to:
   - methods of collecting information to analyse factors impacting performance;

     or
   - approaches to performance development;

     or
   - recording, monitoring and evaluating performance development.
3. Highlight the key information given.
4. Identify the command words used in the question.
5. Begin to answer the questions asked.

Scenario 1

Look at the picture above and answer the questions which follow.

Your answers must make reference to the emotional factor and one other selected from physical, mental or social.

1. Explain how a performance might be negatively affected by factors impacting performance. **(8 marks)**

2. Analyse a course of action which would attempt to develop the factors in part 1. **(8 marks)**

TOP TIP

You must try to relate your skills, knowledge and understanding back to the scenario given.
Simply explaining how *any* performance is negatively affected by the emotional and one other factor will not gain you high marks.
Also, when analysing a course of action you put forward to develop the two factors you have already written about, you must again try to *apply* your plan to the scenario given.

Remember:

Describe means saying things like:	Explain means saying things like:
<ul><li>what a performance looks like;</li><li>what strengths there are in the performance;</li><li>what development needs there are.</li></ul>	<ul><li>because …</li><li>so …</li><li>in order to allow me to …</li><li>to make sure that …</li><li>to provide me with the opporunity to …</li><li>when I needed to …</li></ul>

Analyse means saying things like:	Evaluate means saying things like:
• this shows me that … • this allowed for … • as a result … • this resulted in … • the result of this course of action was … • this meant that …	• demonstrating a significant improvement … • clearly results show … • overall the preferred method would be … because … • the approach most useful was … because …

Scenario 2

	5 mins	10 mins	15mins
Fouls committed	x		
Interceptions	xx		
Successful passes	xxx		
Unsuccessful passes	x	xx	xxxx
Shots on target	xx	xxx	xxxx
Shots off target	xxx	xx	
Possession given away	x	xxx	xxxx

Look at the table above and answer the questions which follow.

Your answers must make reference to the physical factor and one other selected from mental, emotional or social.

1. Analyse the performance throughout the 15-minute period. **(8 marks)**
2. Explain the purpose and value of using data to help develop performance. **(8 marks)**

TOP TIP

You must try to refer to the data in the scenario 'prompt' when analysing the performance. Start at 5 minutes and systematically break down the data in the next two columns to show how performance physically – and perhaps mentally – for poor decision-making when passing, or possible anxiety for emotional, or poor team work for the social factor results in an overall deterioration in all the statistics given.

Glossary of key terms

Bio feedback	A collection of measurements and data from within the body which indicates changes in breathing, heart rate or body temperature.
Environmental checklist	A list of available facilities or resources within a performer's community.
French low serve test	A test which requires the player to try to serve to set target areas where points are awarded and totalled to give an overall score.
General observation schedule	Qualitative method of collecting data on a whole performance.
Illinois agility test	A test for agility which requires the performer to run through cones in a set pattern with the time taken to complete, recorded.
Kinaesthetic feedback	The internal feelings produced when carrying out a performance.
Leger test	A standardised fitness test used to measure cardio-respiratory endurance.
Mind map	A graphic organiser to put together important information in a visual or pictorial way.
Model performer	A performer who is seen to demonstrate the 'ideal' performance to aspire to.
PAR (preparation, action and recovery)	Method of collecting data on a discrete skill.
PDP (performance development plan)	Method of improving areas across one or more factor.
Principles of effective practice	Practices have to be based on model performance criteria, have variety to lessen boredom, be specific to weakness, be progressive and have realistic set targets/goals to be achieved over an agreed time scale.
Principles of training	Specificity, progression, overload, reversibility and tedium – the 'rules' by which a physical fitness programme would be organised.
Protocols	Set rules about how tests should be set up, administered and recorded.
Qualitative	Information which is generally an opinion about the quality of a performance.
Quantitative	Data which can be counted and is less likely to be based on opinion.
Questionnaires	A series of questions where the responses are stored.
Scenario	A performance prompt which outlines a particular set of circumstances.
SMART	Target-setting approach which enables goals to be specific, measurable, achievable, relevant and time set.
The demands of an activity	The requirements in terms of skills, fitness and composition or tactics.
The nature of an activity	The performance context: inside, outside, team/group/individual scoring systems.

Chapter 4: Collecting information to analyse factors impacting on performance

The following are detailed answer frameworks for the Higher exam. You can use these as templates to construct your answers, making them personal to you and the activities you have studied. The missing sections, indicted by '...', are where you should add information related to your own experiences in order to gain the full range of marks available.

Analysing information collection methods (page 36)

1 Compare two different methods of data collection from within one factor

   a Describe the two methods. **(4 marks)**

A general observation schedule (GOS) is a sheet with criteria from a model performance. These are areas from my whole game such as … It has lines and rows, allowing me to tick or cross to indicate whether I can carry out this area of my performance effectively … I use a video to complete this using the rewind and pause facility as I watch different sections of my game … at the end I total the Never, Sometimes and Always columns for each aspect of my game …

The next method is a scattergram, which is a diagram of a bird's eye view of the court … where I record and number where every single service lands on my opponent's side of the net and whether it is a successful shot or not … the cross I mark on the scattergram is circled if it is an outright winner … showing each service which is also numbered … at the end of the game I transfer my data to a sheet which asks for the outcome of every service … it shows where my winners landed and the number of times my serve landed out …

   b Explain what makes them different or more useful. **(4 marks)**

The GOS is a picture of all aspects of my game, whereas the scattergram looks only at the outcome of my service … The scattergram gives quantifiable evidence which can let me … The GOS looks at every single aspect of my game and means I can look for all my strengths and development needs in order to prioritise … The scattergram is easy to read and quickly gives me a summary of …

   c Analyse why one method is better than the other. **(4 marks)**

I think the scattergram is the most useful of the two methods because it gives me evidence of the number of times I get it wrong in a game … It lets me begin a programme of work knowing exactly what part of my game I need to begin to focus on … It gives me target areas to improve as I can be specific about …

d Evaluate the overall reliability of both. **(4 marks)**

Both are reliable as they use video evidence to gather footage for analysis … This means the evidence can be checked and double-checked … Errors are unlikely as the footage and completed paperwork can be revisited by someone else … It is unlikely that the information could be misinterpreted as both are simple tally marks and ticks or crosses … This makes reading and totalling …

Applying recognised tests or analytical tools (page 40)

1 Describe the 'protocol' for a test you have used to gather information on a factor which affects your performance. **(4 marks)**

The Leger Test requires a measured distance of 20m to be marked out. The recorded CD begins and runners begin keeping time with the 'bleeps', trying to reach and turn at the line just before the 'bleep' goes. The bleeps get faster and the runners must keep getting across the line before the 'bleep' … they keep going and the levels are announced by the CD until the runner fails to reach the line twice … the number previous to this is recorded as the score achieved.

2 Explain the advantages of having an experienced observer collect information on your performance. **(4 marks)**

An experienced observer can quickly see faults and errors and, if familiar with the method of recording, can complete the schedule accurately with no time wasted … their experience is likely to allow quick analysis of strengths and areas for development … the performer is likely to take on board feedback from an experienced and knowledgeable observer more readily than from one who has little experience.

3 Justify the need to follow set protocols when gathering information on performance. **(4 marks)**

The protocols need to be followed so that the test is carried out exactly the same way each time it is carried out. This means the laps completed, distance covered or achieved can be calculated accurately … and that comparisons between two sets of results are possible … improvements can be attributed to improved performance and not a shorter test track, for example.

4 Identify two methods you have used to collect information on your performance for different factors. **(2 marks)**

Skills test, questionnaire, scattergrams, apps, observation schedules, match analysis sheets, PAR sheets … Any two.

5 Evaluate the benefits of both methods in enabling you to collect information that allowed you to begin planning performance development. **(6 marks)**

Pacetracker App – The method allows quantifiable evidence to be collected. This is most valuable because it is indisputable, is fact and therefore provides evidence which can be used to set targets for training and for re-testing easily after the training period … It also gives a detailed analysis and a visual picture of the areas covered on the pitch … This is most useful as on re-testing the two sets of stats can easily be compared via the box graph facility of the app … It is quick and straightforward to see the difference in metres covered over the playing period …

The questionnaire is more subjective and perhaps less accurate, as it could be affected by the mood the person is in when completing it … this means the results of the method could be disputed and might not give as accurate a picture of strengths and weaknesses … In effect this means it is less reliable than the Pacetracker app …

Model performances (page 43)

1   Describe a model performance from an activity of your choice.   **(4 marks)**

In trampolining a model performer would be able to stay high on the bed and maintain this height for the entire routine … also, they would stay in the centre of the bed with strong posture and arm and foot positions … their execution of individual skills would be effective and arms and legs would be held appropriately throughout … in a sequence each move would flow into the next and they would make the sequence overall look fluent and controlled …

2   Explain the limitations of comparing your own performance to a model performer who is much better than you.   **(4 marks)**

Sometimes the model performer has a range of skills which would be impossible for me to achieve … the comparison may not therefore be realistic – I might be trying to achieve something which is beyond me … this would affect my motivation and make me give up or not try so hard during my training … progress would then be slow or stop altogether …

3   Evaluate the differences between the model performer's management of emotions and your own in a stressful performance situation.   **(4 marks)**

The model performer's management of emotions during a hockey game should be effective in all situations throughout a performance … even when they tire … they would not lose their control and react inappropriately … also, in stressful situations they would not get upset or lose confidence in their ability, allowing them to carry out the performance to a consistently high standard … on the other hand, when I get tired, I tend to make rash challenges and have on occasion been red-carded as I react badly to contact from my opponent … I feel I can't cope with the demands of the performance and I end up giving up or not chasing back because I feel frustrated that there is no point.

4   Analyse the model performer's ability to make effective decisions within a performance situation.   **(4 marks)**

The model performer in rugby will see what decision needs to be taken and will carry through with the right option … this will result in them keeping possession … or getting possession … mistakes will not be made and overall the performance will be successful … he will control each part of his performance effectively by analysing the options which are available in each situation and choosing the correct one … points would be won … possession denied and confidence would be high as a result …

Interpreting qualitative and quantitative, and objective information (page 46)

1 Describe the qualitative information you gathered for a factor of your choice. **(4 marks)**

In badminton I got qualitative information from my PAR sheet ... this indicated over a number of shots which part of my weak stroke was giving me most problems ... it highlighted that in the action phase I was slow to get my weight from back to front foot and that my arm was not straight as I struck the shuttle ... also the point of contact when hitting the shuttle was above my head and not in front of it ...

2 Explain how a combination of quantitative and qualitative information gives you a useful picture of performance. **(4 marks)**

Qualitative information gives the 'colour' to the performance picture ... it is more than hard facts and if a visual picture can be included via photograph or video footage and then combined with statistics about how many times the wrong technique was used then the performer has a great deal of information to use to begin performance development ... quantitative evidence combined with the qualitative information can be vital in checking for improvements after a programme of work ... the correct technique can be viewed and assessed by people watching and giving opinions (qualitative data), but knowing the number of points won (quantitative data) is a useful 'back up' or additional piece of proof about how much better the weak technique is ...

3 Analyse the impact of subjective opinions upon a development plan. **(4 marks)**

Personal opinions can encourage a performer to alter what they are doing ... if they feel progress is slow they might think it a good idea to increase the intensity of the training being completed ... this would mean the training would progress and performance improve ... opinions from someone other than the performer might lead a development plan to go in another direction and would be dependent on how valid the opinions were ... this could positively or even negatively impact on the training being completed as the performer might be doing training which becomes too hard, too easy or even be inappropriate for them ...

4 Evaluate the quality of the information you gathered after completing your performance development plan. **(4 marks)**

The quality of evidence gathered was useful because it gave me an update on my current level based on comparison between previous tests ... the information was accurate and I could rely on it to begin to plan performance development ... this was because the conditions under which it was gathered were exactly the same as the first time ... it gave me clear data about the number of times I got it wrong ... providing me with factual data to check for improvements ...

Receiving/accepting/giving/timing feedback (page 52)

1   Describe two types of feedback.   **(4 marks)**

Internal feedback is that feeling a performer gets when they carry out a skill ... how well they strike the shuttle or ball, how securely they land from a jump, how controlled the turn is, how much power is put into a pass to make it reach a teammate ...

Visual feedback is in the form of a video where a performer would be recorded and then allowed to see the footage of herself in action ... this might also be paused to show specific skills or instances in a performance which should be the focus for performance development ...

2   Analyse the impact of the feedback you received on your level of arousal.   **(4 marks)**

At a break between games my coach told me that it appeared I wasn't involved in the first 5 mins of the game ... this made me feel very guilty as I knew I had gone on with the wrong attitude and had not worked hard to begin with ... internal feedback while I was playing told me that I felt out of my depth, fearful that the opponent was much better than me and that I couldn't match her range of shots or power ... this made me hesitate to carry out my game plan of forcing her to the back of the court and using my OHC as a building shot to tire her out and keep her from smashing ...

3   Evaluate your willingness to receive feedback from another member of your class.
   (4 marks)

Sometimes I don't listen properly to the feedback my partner gives ... this is because I'm not sure she is being serious ... there are also times when I think she just says anything about my sequence, which might not be accurate, and so I don't trust what it is that she is trying to tell me ... I don't think she knows enough about the sport to be able to teach me anything and so I just ignore her advice ...

4   Explain the importance of timing feedback when developing performance.   **(4 marks)**

Feedback needs to be given as soon after a performance as possible so that the performance is fresh in the performer's mind ... Feedback during a performance, by calling a time out or between sets or attempts, means there is the chance to change or adjust things to get a better overall result ... it is also necessary to time feedback at crucial parts of learning, for example at the cognitive stage when lots of ongoing feedback can help a performer reduce basic, fundamental errors, which would stop them building a good foundation to progress with their learning ...

Chapter 5: Approaches to performance development

Purpose of performance development planning (Page 55)

1   Describe a plan for improving a factor of your choice.   **(4 marks)**

Physical factor – use a running programme three times per week, using a variety of types of running specific to my activity … interval, Fartlek and continuous … keep heart in training zone for at least 20 mins … progressing training by increasing intensity by … duration by … or frequency by …

Mental – for dance, do a programme of mental rehearsal to try to improve my decision-making skills in the performance situation … start with learning the technique of mentally running through in my mind the situations which give me most trouble in the routine … break the dance down into the beginning/starting positions and first 16 count sequence … run through in my mind the counts and specifically the first step onto the left foot … rehearsing this start phase I then move onto the section after the pairs section where I wait and count 6 beats before I join in on the right-hand side of my partner, taking her left hand … I count the beats, close my eyes and see myself stepping forward to the side and firmly and confidently taking my partner's hand and turning in perfect time with the music, ready to complete the next part of the sequence side by side …

Emotional and social – use restorative practices to help players in my team understand the implications of losing control of their emotions and the impact this has on team cohesion. Start by asking our former captain, who has retired from playing to be the mediator … get the group together and ask them to give one word which would illustrate how we felt after a specific match which we lost and where we all ended up arguing … don't allow anyone to comment on what is said and keep our eyes on the mediator and not the other players … write the list of words on a flipchart as they are said and put them under the heading positive or negative … pair up and tell the other person the best thing about being in this team … list these on the flip chart and group them together into similar themes … talk though what happens when a team doesn't pull together … suggest a few strategies for the team to try over the coming weeks to put all the negative things behind us … plan a feedback session after the next game but don't make negative comments during the game … only the Captain to be allowed to give instructions …

2   Explain why a plan must be specific to your needs.   **(6 marks)**

A plan needs to suit personal needs so that the areas requiring attention are concentrated on and improved … a plan needs to match the current level of skill or fitness so that steady, progressive steps in the development process can be taken gradually and sensibly … a plan which is not matched to specific needs will have a negative effect on motivation and confidence levels – the performer must feel challenged while working but not so challenged that they feel it is impossible to achieve the required targets … if the plan doesn't consider the demands of the activity then it will not have the desired effect and there will be no positive impact on the performance …

3 Explain how you could use data to effectively plan for performance development.

(4 marks)

Data is useful in finding a starting point for training to begin … it allows targets to be set which enable gradual, safe, productive training … data provides a motivational tool, as progress can be measured and observed, which might spur on further effort and hard work … data allows clearly identified priorities … in that the area with most crosses on an observation schedule will be the one which will become the focus for performance development … data from before training and after training can be compared to check for improvements and thereby establish the effectiveness of approaches being used …

4 Evaluate how successful your planning was for your exams last year.   **(4 marks)**

I was successful in planning for my history exam as I achieved an A in the final exam and I felt confident going into the exam … I knew every topic on the paper and there was no area which I was unable to answer – my component mark showed that I had achieved 52 out of the available marks in the paper … I was less successful in my chemistry exam where I only received a C pass. I had found some of the topics challenging and instead of asking for help, I decided not to study them in the hope they didn't come up – they did and there were 14 marks I wrote nothing for on the paper out of 60 … this was reflected in my grade … In PE I had focused on all four factors and my training approaches for each of them … I achieved an A pass and in the marks available from school I could see that I had done well, achieving 35 of the 40 marks … my planning to study the week before each of the exams helped me prioritise and prepare fully the two days before … this meant the knowledge was fresh in my mind on the day of the exam …

Prioritising development needs (page 59)

1 Explain why a sound aerobic base is useful before work begins on other aspects of fitness.   **(4 marks)**

The aerobic base is the foundation upon which all other aspects of training are established … by having effective heart and lungs, all other types of training are more effective … the aerobic base allows for good transportation of oxygen around the body, meaning weights, sprinting, plyometrics, circuits are likely to be more productive … the aerobic base is like the building block at the bottom of a pyramid – on which all other aspects of fitness can be built …

2 Describe the difficulties lack of concentration might give a team or group when just one person does not listen.   **(4 marks)**

If one person misses important instructions about what to do then there is a weak link in the team or group who will not carry out their designated role effectively … letting the rest of the group down … exposing gaps … if one person does not mark who they should then there is likely to be an overload situation, meaning someone has more than one person to defend against … in a dance, if one group member does not get the correct place to lift another dancer, then the dance will look messy and cause confusion with the other dancers …

3 Identify the type of development plan which has more than one factor as its focus.

(1 mark)

An **integrated programme** has more than one area of development as its focus.

4   Explain why training priorities must be based on information collected.   **(4 marks)**

If training priorities are based on guesses and not information then it is likely progress in terms of overall performance development will be limited, as the training completed might not be necessary or appropriate … if training is not based on information gathered then injury might occur as no clear, safe starting point will have been established … training priorities must be personal and agreed with the performer otherwise personal commitment might not be given to the work being completed …

Potential impacts of factors on performance development (page 63)

1   Explain how the mental factor might affect your performance development plan process.   **(4 marks)**

Poor concentration might affect the performer while they are carrying out their development plan, e.g. they might lose focus and not complete the circuit, drill, approach correctly and therefore will not see the benefit … different levels of arousal might affect a performer, as they might not be interested in working hard and so again the progress they make would be limited as they would only 'get out what they put in' … this means motivation levels to see the training through to the end of the development plan might not exist and a performer might give up halfway through …

2   Describe the challenges the social factor might have on performance development.   **(4 marks)**

Training as part of a group or on your own is a matter of individual preference … however, if you work harder when you are with a training buddy than when completing training on your own, then it would be wise to always organise training with another person … this person must be as determined, or more determined, than you to work hard … that way you are more likely to complete the session … if your 'buddy' is lazy and encourages you to slow down or cheat, then their presence is unhelpful … You may prefer a person of the same sex to train with you … that way the physical differences would not be an issue … e.g. you can potentially run as fast as someone of the same sex, but possibly not against a performer of the opposite sex …

3   Explain how you could use positive self-talk to help you get into the right frame of mind to complete a session of your performance development plan.   **(4 marks)**

Before beginning the programme, I would look back at my training diary and see how far I've come, how much progress I've made … I'd say to myself that I'd done well so far and that today was another step along the road to success … this would help me go into training positive and motivated … I'd tell myself it was going to be difficult and hard work but that the reward would be worth it … this would make me ready for the challenges of the session … I'd warm up thoroughly, telling myself to treat each part of the warm-up as preparation for a worthwhile session without injury … during the session – especially when I wanted to give up – I'd repeat to myself 'hard work brings results' … this would encourage me to push through …

4   Explain what evidence you might gather to show you are managing the impact of the four factors on performance. **(4 marks)**

A range of evidence would be gathered to show that the impact of physical fitness, skills, tactics, mental, emotional and social factors was positive and manageable within a performance, e.g. physical – evidence would show if a performer was managing to maintain the same performance level at the beginning compared to the end of the performance … this would indicate stamina levels were effective … mental – lack of concentration would show in evidence about the number of times a marker lost their opponent … this would indicate a lapse in concentration … emotional – evidence from a disciplinary record would show that a performer had lost control of their temper and had picked up fouls … social – in early stages of a game poor levels of co-operation would be evidenced by passes being intercepted and a lack of support for players running back to cover in a defensive situation …

Performance development goals (page 66)

1   Describe two goals you have set. **(2 marks)**

A short-term goal would be to improve my landing from a handspring onto two feet without taking a step forward by the end of the training session … a long-term goal would be to add a twist to my back somersault within my sequence by the end of the season, or a new sequence at a different level of difficulty next season.

2   Explain why these goals are relevant to you. **(4 marks)**

The goals are about things I need to do to make my own performance better … they are specific to improve areas of my performance … they must be able to motivate me to keep working towards my overall aim of improving my performance …

3   Explain why we need a variety of goals when we are working to develop performance **(4 marks)**

Goals need to be focused on what is to be done to that specific performance, i.e. the outcome of the performance – to win or to be successful … you know what action has to be taken in order for you to win or be successful … goals motivate a performer to keep going … even when success has not been achieved … In a challenging performance process, goals can help a performer remain focused, sticking to their game plan even when it seems it is not bringing about the desired results …

4   Describe the three types of goals. **(3 marks)**

Outcome goal *– to win today's match … what has to be done in this one performance situation …*

Process goal *– can be used to help you achieve an outcome goal … using your best techniques effectively to help you overcome an opponent.*

Performance goal *– can be used to check progress towards achieving process goals … so comparing success within the performance with a previous performance will highlight how close you are to achieving a goal.*

5 Describe the three types of goals. **(3 marks)**

Outcome goal – to win today's match … what has to be done in this one performance situation …

Process goal – can be used to help you achieve an outcome goal … using your best techniques effectively to help you overcome an opponent.

Performance goal – can be used to check progress towards achieving process goals … so comparing success within the performance with a previous performance will highlight how close you are to achieving a goal.

Approaches to meet performance development goals (page 71)

1 Describe one approach you have used within a personal development plan. **(2 marks)**

Physical – the skill development programme in badminton would begin with shadowing where there would be no movement … no shuttle … simply the performer standing still, shadowing (mirroring marks) the weak stroke … then movement might be added on, where the performer would move from base position to play the imaginary shuttle … from there repetition drills might be used, where a predictable feed would be given time after time to the performer who was standing waiting to play the shuttle from the area where the shuttle was being fed from … then the feed would become unpredictable … then conditioned games would be built in, where there would be an extra point given if the rally were won by playing the stroke which was being developed.

Mental – I would use deep breathing by sitting at the side of the gym, closing my eyes and taking in deep, slow breaths for 3 minutes. Each breath should be taken in slowly – I should feel the whole of my chest being filled with air. The breath should be held for 8–10 seconds and then slowly blown out through the nose … The eyes should remain closed and while this is happening, my only focus should be the breathing process … all other distractions, thoughts and concerns should be removed from my mind …

Emotional – a team talk would take the form of the captain organising to speak with the group … she would start by telling us things which had gone well in the previous game and then she would tell us who was to play where and what we were expected to do in our positions and at set pieces … she would try to motivate us to work together and to see the importance of supporting each other when in attack and defence.

Social – active listening techniques would be organised where we would split into two groups and then sit in two circles, facing someone in our group … one person after another would introduce themselves and say which school they came from and which position they play … we would then move round to the next person and introduce the player we had just met to a new player … this would continue until each player had met one new player and introduced one other player to the group … we would then have 3 minutes to try to speak to every other player in the group and listen and recount their information to the whole group …

2   Explain the need for specificity when choosing an approach to develop performance.

(4 marks)

An approach has to be specific to a performer so that it matches the individual needs of the performer in terms of their strengths and weaknesses … this makes sure the approach matches the needs identified … it also has to match the demands of the performance context so that, after working on a development need, it can be reintegrated/put back into the performance situation and be used … this also means the skill being worked on has to be practised under the same conditions that are required in a live performance context … in terms of physical fitness, the muscle groups being used in a sport need to be the focus of training so that when back in the live performance situation, the muscle groups most needed have been developed … in mental and emotional approaches, the context where the approach is to be used must be considered, e.g. a performer can't stop to visualise their shot on goal in open play … therefore the approach chosen to control nerves would need to be able to be used just as the shot was taken …

3   Analyse two approaches you have used within a personal development plan.   **(4 marks)**

Analysis shown in red.

Mental – I would use deep breathing by sitting at the side of the gym, closing my eyes and taking in deep, slow breaths for 3 minutes, each breath should be slowly taken in and I should feel the whole of my chest being filled with air. This would allow me to begin shutting out all noises and my surroundings bit by bit, and to take control of my mind. The breath should be held for 8–10 seconds and then slowly blown out through the nose; as a result I would feel totally in control of my thoughts since I would only be focusing on the 10-second countdown … the eyes should remain closed … this would result in a calm, controlled feeling inside where I was totally managing my thoughts and not letting anything distract me from the breathing. While this was happening my only focus would be the breathing process … all other distractions, thoughts and concerns should be removed from my mind. As a result, I would finish ready to focus on the dance routine and not the confusion I had been feeling before I began my deep breathing …

Social – active listening techniques would be organised, where we would split into two groups and then sit in two circles facing someone in our group. This means that we would have to sit opposite someone we don't know very well and so might not have chosen to talk to … one after the other each person should introduce themselves and says which school they come from and which position they play. This would act as an ice breaker and give us something to say in this situation, when we might have struggled to start a conversation … we would then move round to the next person and introduce the person we had just met to this new person. This would allow us not to speak about ourselves, which might be a little awkward – instead someone else would speak for us … this would continue until each person had met one person and then introduced one other person to the group … we would then have 3 minutes to try to speak to every other person in the group and listen and recount their information to the whole group … this would result in the group relaxing and feeling less self-conscious and more willing to communicate with each other.

4   Explain how you would evaluate the effectiveness of one of your chosen approaches.

(4 marks)

Evaluation shown in red.

Emotional – a team talk would take the form of the captain organising to speak with the group. This made a positive impact right from the beginning as we knew exactly who was in charge and this meant no one felt they could or should offer opinions about what we could or should do … she would start by telling us things which had gone well the game before. This started the meeting off very positively and got people listening and encouraged them to get into a positive mindset; and then she would tell us who was to play where and what we were expected to do in our positions and at set pieces. Because we were all listening and had been told what had gone well in the last game we took on board her instructions, meaning there was no confusion and we were all extremely clear about what was expected of us … she would try to motivate us to work together and to see the importance of supporting each other when in attack and defensively. This was useful as she left each of us feeling our role was important and that we were valued. This sent us off to play determined and optimistic about winning …

Chapter 6: Recording, monitoring and evaluating performance development

Purpose and value of recording, monitoring and evaluating performance development (page 75)

1 Describe one method used to monitor performance development. **(4 marks)**

A training diary can be used to monitor the ongoing progress of your performance. The diary would be completed by the performer straight after the performance … It would enable the performer to complete key information such as the date, time, success of the performance and development needs of the performance … There would be an opportunity to complete a next steps section …

2 Compare the work you completed at the beginning of your personal development plan to that at the end of the plan. **(4 marks)**

During my PDP I completed several sessions of Progressive Muscular Relaxation techniques to help with my anxiety levels. During my initial session I had to really concentrate on relaxing my muscles step by step and had to take my time … As the sessions went on I was able to relax my muscles quicker and felt the response.

This benefited my PDP, as initially I had to really concentrate on the technique so that I got it right and it led to my anxiety levels being reduced, however this took up a lot of …

3 Analyse the evidence your monitoring methods generated which indicated it was necessary to change or adapt your personal development plan. **(4 marks)**

Being able to compare my observation schedule every two weeks allowed me to specifically pinpoint the areas in my performance and approaches that needed to be developed or adapted … this quantitative evidence gave me reliable facts, showing …

4 Evaluate the progress you made on completion of your development plan. **(4 marks)**

I feel from what can be seen in both my monitoring methods that an improvement has been made. From my training diary, I can see that I felt quite tired at the initial sessions, however, from my subjective statements at the end of my PDP I can see that I was able to complete the sessions with less fatigue, and during my performance I was able to keep up with my opponent with more success. Quantitative evidence from my fitness tests show that I have increased my Leger test by 2 levels, showing that …

This increase in aerobic endurance allowed me to last the whole length of my performance without my skill level movement patterns deteriorating.

Key planning information (page 78)

1 Describe the most important piece of planning information you used. **(4 marks)**

During my planning I felt it was crucial to set targets which were SMART … My target was specific to my performance and level of ability … I was able to measure whether I was achieving my target or not … My target was realistically something I could achieve over the period of time I would set my PDP for … I also needed to make sure that I had the appropriate amount of time to achieve my target.

A description of how you applied the principles of **training** and/or **effective practice** before commencing your PDP may also be used.

2 Explain the planning information you made use of to organise your PDP. **(4 marks)**

I used my planning information to make sure I set a PDP which was specific to my needs and that would progressively challenge the area that I needed to develop. By setting a target that was SMART I was able to organise my PDP with approaches which best suited my development needs. For example, I used interval training and Fartlek training as this allowed me to specifically work on my aerobic endurance so that I … I also considered the use of principles of training when planning my PDP. This allowed me to set my PDP at the appropriate level at the various stages. I was therefore able to progressively overload my PDP so that my aerobic endurance was always being challenged and increased.

3 Analyse the use of goal-setting within planning for performance development. **(4 marks)**

During planning for my PDP I analysed my use of goal setting by breaking down goals and ensuring they were SMART. I felt it was crucial to set targets which were SMART … My target was specific to my performance and level of ability … I was able to measure whether I was achieving my target or not … My target was something I could realistically achieve over the period of time I would set my PDP for … I also needed to make sure that I had the appropriate amount of time to achieve my target.

4 Evaluate the accuracy of your key planning information. **(4 marks)**

At the end of each session and my PDP, I was able to form a judgement as to whether my key planning information, such as my goal-setting, was having the outcome I expected. At the end of each session, I compared my thoughts and feelings about how I felt I was meeting my goals and compared this information to prior sessions. This allowed me to gain subjective information directly related to my goals, e.g. the repetition drill allowed me to practise the small errors that were still occurring in my overhead clear, as this was one of my key targets …

Recording and monitoring methods or tools (page 81)

1 Describe a method to monitor the impact of a Social factor. **(4 marks)**

I used a training diary to monitor the impact communication was having on my performance. I completed my diary straight after each session was completed to develop my communication as a centre in netball. This allowed me to write down my own opinions and feelings in a diary. I noted key information, such as the date, time, success of the session and performance and my next development needs to further enhance my communication … There was an opportunity to complete a next steps section …

2 Explain the importance of monitoring your personal development programme. **(4 marks)**

I monitored my PDP by using a training diary and by comparing information I received from a questionnaire throughout my PDP. I was able to gain subjective information on whether the approaches used within my PDP were having a positive effect. This then allowed me to adapt or change parts of my PDP, so that I was always seeking to improve. By using these methods to monitor I was able to continually check progress and, by having two forms of monitoring, I was able to make sure the information was more reliable, so that I could check this information against my goals.

3 Analyse the effectiveness of the method selected. **(4 marks)**

I used two monitoring methods – a questionnaire and a training diary. The training diary was broken down into sub-headings which gave me direction as to the types of information I needed to record. However, this was quite general and was based on my own opinion. The questionnaire allowed me to consider the specific questions related to both my PDP and my performance, which meant I could focus a lot more on what was being asked and give more specific responses. This led to a more reliable source of information, which gave me more reliable details as to how I could make changes over the course of my PDP.

Production and implementation of performance development plans (page 84)

1 Describe SMART targets that could be set to develop the Physical factor. **(4 marks)**

These would be specific to the area of weakness, for example to improve my speed over a short distance … and also measurable, e.g. I would want to improve my speed by 0.5 seconds over 50 metres … this improvement is only 0.5 seconds over an 8-week training programme and is achievable and realistic for this training period … I've set myself a time-frame of 8 weeks to check for improvements.

2 Explain why these targets are SMART. **(4 marks)**

Explanation in red.

These would be specific to the area of weakness, for example to improve my speed over a short distance. This is an area within my game which lets me down, e.g. I struggle to beat opponents to a 50/50 ball and so am always trying to chase back to regain possession for my team … also measurable, e.g. I want to improve my speed by 0.5 seconds over 50 metres, so I am able to measure any improvements in my time achieved … this will indicate whether I have made any progress with my speed training … this improvement is only 0.5 seconds over an 8-week training programme and is achievable and realistic for me in this training period. If I had set myself a 5-second target for improvement, this would be almost impossible in the time available for a performer like me … I have kept my focus, as I feel the target is something I will be able to achieve with hard work … this drives me to keep going … I've set myself a time frame of 8 weeks to then check for improvements … this is enough time to see a difference and yet it's not so long that I might lose interest and motivation.

3 What principles do you need to consider to develop a fitness PDP? **(4 marks)**

The principles of training need to be considered when organising a PDP for fitness. Specificity is required to ensure the programme of work and approaches used match the performance; the performer's needs and the context of the activity would need to be considered too … Progressive overload is also a principle which needs to be applied, as the body goes through its adaptation process … this is applied by altering the frequency – the number of sessions done in a week or by applying intensity – making the training harder/pushing the body to do more than it is used to doing or by making the session duration last longer.

4 Describe methods of monitoring the PDP. **(4 marks)**

Monitoring can take place through keeping notes of training completed and feelings and opinions about each session … this can be recorded in a diary with headings for when training was done, what training was completed, how the performer felt during and after the session and also the plan for the next session … Also by re-testing mid-way through, the training progress can be monitored by comparing the results …

5 Compare pre- and post-PDP evaluations of your performance. **(4 marks)**

Before training my CRE level in the Leger test was Level 22 … after training my test results showed a huge improvement to level 48. This is more than 100% improvement and shows that my training clearly has benefited me … in my game I am able to last until the 64th minute before I feel tired as compared to my pre-PDP results … again this indicates a significant improvement in the way I felt while playing … this indicates my stamina has risen and I am lasting until 85 mins before I begin to feel tired … my stats show too that, even after 85 minutes, I am still passing accurately and remaining focused marking my opponent. This is in contrast to my pre-PDP stats, which showed that I lost focus and therefore my opponent many times before the 35th minute …

Adapting performance development plans (page 87)

1 Describe two ways you adapted your PDP. **(4 marks)**

I adapted my plan by changing the key words I would use for different situations in a game during practice … I used only three words but each was used in different situations … key word one was to be used before I pushed the ball out at the corner … I said 'target' just as I put my stick in position and looked at the person I was going to pass to … the second key word was 'recovery', which I said just before taking a free hit to encourage me to allow my stick to follow through as I hit the ball, increasing the accuracy of my pass … thirdly, as I ran back into defence I said 'chase' as I caught up and either tackled or closed down the person with the ball … The second way I adapted my PDP was by allowing my captain to use a key word to encourage me to control my emotions during the practice games … she would call 'focus' when she had witnessed me either giving up or perhaps getting angry after a failed tackle or pass …

2   Explain which of the two adaptations was most challenging.   **(4 marks)**

The adaptation of using my captain to 'call me' was the most challenging, as she had to know me well and make sure she only used the key word when she could see me 'losing it' – this prevented her overusing it and meant I responded appropriately because I would react to her call, doing what she wanted me to do … it was also challenging as my instincts were to answer back or complain when she called me for giving up while chasing back … however, because I really respected her, I didn't do so …

3   Analyse the effect of the changes to your PDP on your level of motivation.   **(4 marks)**

As I was doing something different and could see the benefits and positive impact of the changes I had made, my motivation increased … I was able to chase back much more often. Hearing my captain 'call me' when she wanted me to 'dig in' and chase back, or shout 'well done' and 'good job' motivated me and seemed to also increase my energy levels and enthusiasm to play on even when I was tired …

4   Evaluate the success of the changes you made to your PDP.   **(4 marks)**

I was successful when changing some things about my PDP … the evidence shows that I won nine out of eleven possible tackles … this compares favourably with my previous match where I won only one out of eight … this demonstrated clearly that my motivation had increased … I also felt better…I felt energised and able to carry on, as mentally I did feel I was doing a good job and that my contributions were valued by the team …

Future performance development planning (page 89)

1   Compare your pre- and post-training performances.   **(4 marks)**

Before training I was described as the weak link in my group when it came to handling pressure … I would get nervous before I went on to perform and so when the ball came at me from a quick service I would hesitate or be too upright and not 'cushion' the ball into my setter … now, after training, I have controlled my nerves and I am key in getting the ball accurately into the setter and we build attacks sometimes from the very first attack … I am also able to help other players settle, as my calm approach seems to have a positive impact on the players around me … they are inspired to stay focused and to help cover for others, which again really builds team confidence and reduces stress and anxiety …

2   Explain why you have prioritised your future development need.   **(4 marks)**

I have lots of training needs but I have identified one – my backhand – which will have the biggest impact on my overall performance … I need to reflect on where I am now, then after training, and from there move on to the next area which is in need of attention … this will probably be something which has come to light as a result of training I have been doing and could also be something which if ignored would stop me making further progress while developing my performance …

3   Analyse the impact of this 'new' development need on your performance.   **(4 marks)**

My backhand gives me problems as 8 out of 10 times I send the shuttle into the net, out of court or 'gift' it to my opponent, who is able to smash and win every point when I am forced to play it … I try to 'run round' my backhand and this causes me to tire very easily and results in my chasing the shuttle around the court … this means I am often not returning to base after playing the shuttle and the opponent is able to exploit spaces I leave … this loses me more points and I end up feeling I have no control over the game … this makes my motivation levels drop and I feel like giving up …

The scenario question (pages 91–92)

Scenario 1

1   Explain how a performance might be negatively affected by factors impacting performance.   **(8 marks)**

Performance might be negatively affected by a performer's lack of control of her emotions. This could mean she gets upset too easily and gives herself a hard time when a mistake is made, which can further affect her ability to keep control. By being too self-critical, the performer might 'tighten up' or become too tense to use a fluent throwing action for her serve. This could mean that the ball might not go up high enough or even in the right direction, resulting in the ball being in an incorrect position to carry out an effective, point-winning serve. If she keeps getting this throw up wrong, then it's possible her emotions could further spiral out of control and result in other parts of her game deteriorating. For example, if playing a serve-and-volley strategy, the service could land shorter than she had anticipated, giving her less time to get into the net and allowing the opponent to play a cross-court punching shot to win the point. Her emotions could also make her react angrily to losing points, which may contribute to her losing further self-control, focus and concentration. This could lead to the performer losing easy points and not seeing spaces or opportunities to exploit her opponent.

For the social factor, in doubles, the same player might end up falling out with her partner, as she feels under pressure from all her mistakes. This would result in poor communication, e.g. both of them going for the same ball or one player thinking the other should go for it. The end result might be neither of them going for the ball and the opposition winning easy points. This would lead to the pair feeling demoralised and perhaps doubting their understanding of their roles in the partnership. This would lead to further confusion and lack of clear decision making, where both players could argue with one other and take the focus off winning. The pair would have little control of the game and could hand control over to the opposition. The opposition may then go from strength to strength, dictating and exhausting the opposition by placing shots just within reach of both players so that neither are able to be confident of who should take the shot.

2   Analyse a course of action which would attempt to develop the factors in part 1. **(8 marks)**

To control emotions the player could carry out a programme of work using trigger words. This would involve using certain chosen words to control emotions when it was likely that the player was going to lose self-control. The player would start by identifying a word which she would say to herself when she felt as though her emotions were running high. In a practice situation, she would instantly say the word to bring herself back into focus and to divert attention away from how she was feeling emotionally. This results in the player changing the thought process from what she feels emotionally to focusing on the word instead. The brain is tricked into changing its point of focus from uncontrollable feelings, to deliberately thinking about this trigger word. This allows the brain and not emotions to be in control of the body and can result in emotions being quickly brought back under control. The player would then be able to more effectively play her game.

For the social factor, a partnership could use the 'positive feedback only' (PFO) approach. In practice games the pair would have one or two phrases like 'never mind, well tried' or 'next shot' which they would use when one or the other made a mistake. As soon as possible after the mistake was made, they would quickly turn to face one other and say their PFO phrase. Players who are used to playing together know what the other needs to hear and this teamwork relationship means they can help each other in points of crisis within a game to quickly re-establish who is doing what or going where. The result of using these PFO phrases is that players see it as part of their responsibility to help others in a team situation – this approach means that players should never feel isolated or unsure of themselves or how their partner or team members feel about them. They are therefore free to concentrate on what their role is in that team. Fear of making mistakes does not make the player freeze up and so, by constantly being encouraged by the PFO, they have more chance of working together in a strong partnership to overcome the opponents.

Scenario 2

1 Analyse the performance throughout the 15-minute period.   **(8 marks)**

The performer's overall success changed as the game went on. In the early stages she made the only foul. This could have been due to a lack of agility, where she may have rushed into a tackle to try to win the ball but perhaps wasn't in the correct position to get her stick on the ground. She made only two interceptions in the first five minutes, and none in the remaining ten minutes, and again this could be attributed to poor timing, where she may not have been able to time her movement to cut off passes within the opposition. Her own passing was relatively unsuccessful – she made only three passes – all of them in the first five minutes and then no successful passes at all for the remainder of the playing period. This is shown by the number of unsuccessful passes rising from one in the first third to two in the second and then finally four in the final third of the game. If the physical factor was affecting her play, it's likely that a lack of skill/technique in the early phase of the game contributed to her making mistakes and giving away possession. Fatigue this early in the game would not have had an impact on her execution of passing. However, fatigue as a result of poor CRE might explain why she gave away the ball more as the game progressed. This is supported by the number of times she gave away possession. The table shows this increases from one occasion in the first five minutes to four occasions in the last third. This could be attributed to poor CRE, as tiredness would make muscles heavy and unable to carry out the correct technique. Poor LME might explain this deterioration, as the muscle groups responsible for getting the stick to repeat the hitting action might be overtired and unable to produce the correct technique to achieve a successful pass.

In terms of the mental factor, her techniques could have been affected by poor concentration due to muscle fatigue. This would mean she was not concentrating properly on what she had to do and reverting to bad or lazy technique. Here, accuracy could therefore suffer and she might give the ball away unnecessarily. Poor decision making also seems be an issue, as in the last third she had no shots on or off target. It's likely that indecision might have crept into her game and she might have decided to stay in defence instead of moving up field to shoot at goal.

Again, this would be explained by poor CRE, as the physical and mental factors are very closely linked. When in the last third she gave away more possession than in all of the previous thirds, it seems possible that this was due to a lack of focus on where she was meant to be playing or even what her role was. She could have lost her opponent, given up or generally failed to be in the right place at the right time. The team would therefore be playing a 'man down' effectively, making it difficult for her teammates to cover all of the opposition players and to stop them scoring goals.

2   Explain the purpose and value of using data to help develop performance.   **(8 marks)**

By using data, such as that provided in the table, it is easy to see areas of a game that are affected by poor CRE, LME or even agility. This allows performers to set targets to improve, as they can see their starting points and then, as they move through a programme of work, keep a check on the progress they are making. This enables performers to reset targets to ensure a steady and continuously progressive training programme. For CRE, targets would need to be set at a level which would allow them to make progress, but at the same time provide challenge to the body so that it could adapt and get fitter. By revisiting the data gathered, performers can see where they've been, the progress made and the next steps they need to take to make sure progress is always positive. If data was not used to set targets effectively, then injury is possible as the targets might force the body to work at a level it is not capable of coping with. Data can also allow performers to see if the effect of improved CRE is carried over into their game. By looking at the data from before and after training, the number of successful tackles, passes, interceptions, etc. are good indicators of improved CRE. This would motivate performers to keep training, as they would they feel better about their performance and be able to contribute more throughout the entire match. This means their team would all be contributing effectively for the entire match with no weak links.

For the mental factor, data can show how lack of concentration affects performers' play and the number of times poor concentration had an impact on interceptions or shots on target. This would provide hard evidence to illustrate how often performers are affected in this way. This would mean that, after training, the approaches used could be examined to see if they actually did what they were meant to. The approach could then be adapted or changed to bring about better results. Mental skills could be further improved by changing the approach, and there might be fewer instances of the performer losing concentration as a result, and giving the ball away or making fewer shots off target. This would increase the chances of the team winning, as more players having shots on target gives a higher percentage of opportunities to score.

© 2015 Leckie & Leckie Ltd
Cover © ink-tank and associates

001/25082015

10 9 8 7 6 5 4 3

ISBN 9780007554416

Published byLeckie & Leckie Ltd
An imprint of HarperCollinsPublishers
Westerhill Road, Bishopbriggs, Glasgow, G64 2QT
T: 0844 576 8126   F: 0844 576 8131
leckieandleckie@harpercollins.co.uk
www.leckieandleckie.co.uk

Commissioning Editor: Fiona Burns
Project manager: Craig Balfour and Keren McGill

Special thanks to
Helen Bleck (copy edit)
Louise Robb (proofread)
Lauren Reid (image research)
QBS (layout)

Printed and bound by CPI Group (UK) Ltd, Croydon, CR0 4YY

A CIP Catalogue record for this book is available from the British Library.

Acknowledgements

P5 Paolo Bona / Shutterstock.com; P6 bibiphoto / Shutterstock.com; P11 Aspen Photo / Shutterstock.com; P12a Gines Romero / Shutterstock.com; P12b Maxisport / Shutterstock.com; P13 Rena Schild / Shutterstock.com; P14 Lilyana Vynogradova / Shutterstock.com; P16 Stephen Dunn / Getty Images; P17b Clive Brunskill / Getty Images; P19 Dziurek / Shutterstock.com; P24 Chris Hellyar / Shutterstock.com; P25 Dziurek / Shutterstock.com; P29b Othman / Shutterstock.com; P29c Jamie Roach / Shutterstock.com; P30b Aspen Photo / Shutterstock.com; P30c FlashStudio / Shutterstock.com; P34 A.RICARDO / Shutterstock.com; P37a Jamie Roach / Shutterstock.com; P37b Corepics VOF / Shutterstock.com; P41b pdrocha / Shutterstock.com; P50 Allison Herreid / Shutterstock.com; P56 BRENDAN SMIALOWSKI/AFP/GettyImages; P57 photofriday / Shutterstock.com; P61a J.M. Eddins Jr. for The Washington Post via Getty Images; P65 Kratky / Shutterstock.com; P68b Cousland / Shutterstock.com; P69 Aspen Photo / Shutterstock.com; P76b muratart / Shutterstock.com; P76c Stefan Holm / Shutterstock.com; P79 Aspen Photo / Shutterstock.com; P80 Maxisport / Shutterstock.com; P85 Kaliva / Shutterstock.com; P86 Maxisport / Shutterstock.com; P88a Brendan Howard / Shutterstock.com; P88b Maxisport / Shutterstock.com; P91 ROSLAN RAHMAN/AFP/Getty Images

Whilst every effort has been made to trace the copyright holders, in cases where this has been unsuccessful, or if any have inadvertently been overlooked, the Publishers would gladly receive any information enabling them to rectify any error or omission at the first opportunity.